GUIDE TO BETTER GARDENING

GALAHAD BOOKS

SHRUBS, TREES AND EVERGREENS

Editor: Margaret Verner
Dust Jacket designed by Roswita Busskamp
Copyright © 1981 by 'Round the World Books Inc.

Shrubs, Trees and Evergreens published by
Galahad Books Inc., New York City.
This edition published by arrangement with
'Round the World Books Inc., New York, N.Y.
Library of Congress Catalog Card Number: 79-56677
ISBN: 0-88365-438-5
Printed in the United States of America

PICTURE ACKNOWLEDGEMENTS:

Augustine Elm Association: 60T — Ball, George J. Inc., West Chicago, Ill.: 67T, 69B — Bristol Nurseries Inc., Bristol, Conn.: 41, 92TL — Bulb Growers Association of Holland: 53T — Canadian Government Travel Bureau, Ottawa, Ont.: 83BR, 86TL — Canadian National Railways: 74T, 74B, 88T — City of Winnipeg: 89BR — Cole Nurseries: 54 — Erindale Nurseries, Erindale, Ont.: 70T — Hamilton, George: 50, 52, 91C, 91R — Horticultural Experiment Station, Vineland, Ont.: 84BR — Kelly Bros., Danville, N.Y.: 53B — McConnell Nurseries: 47, 55R, 80BL, 83TL, 84BL — Morse, A.B.: 6, 7B, 8, 11, 12, 13, 14B, 15BL, 15TL, 16TR, 16B, 17T, 17B, 18T, 18B, 19TL, 19B, 20T, 20B, 21L, 21BR, 22L, 22R, 23L, 24R, 25, 26T, 26B, 27, 28T, 28B, 29T, 29B, 30T, 31TL, 31B, 32B, 33TL, 33B, 34T, 34B, 35, 36T, 36B, 37, 38, 39T, 39B, 40B, 42, 43B, 44T, 46, 48, 51B, 55L, 57, 61, 62T, 64, 65T, 65B, 66T, 66B, 67B, 68, 69T, 70B, 71T, 72B, 75T, 76, 77T, 77B, 78, 81TR, 82R, 87TR, 87B, 90T, 92B, 93TR, 93B, 94L, 95T, 95B, 96L — New Brunswick Dept. of Travel: 49T, 51T, 75B — Nova Scotia Dept. of Travel: 88BR, 89T, 89BL, 90BR — Ontario Agricultural College, Guelph, Ont.: 9BL, 55C, 58B, 60B, 71B, 86TR, 86B, 87TL, 88BL — Ontario Horticultural Association: 49B, 58L, 58C, 72T, 73T, 85B — Patmore Nurseries, Brandon, Manitoba: 84TL, 85T — Press Bureau, Williamsburg, Va.: 23R, 45, 62B — Princeton Nurseries, Princeton, N.J.: 59 — Province of Quebec, Dept. of Travel: 73B — Royal Botanical Gardens, Hamilton, Ont.: 96R — Sheridan Nurseries, Islington, Ont.: 5, 7T, 9T, 10B, 10TL, 10TR, 14T, 15TR, 16TL, 19TR, 21TR, 24L, 30B, 31TR, 32T, 33TR, 40T, 43T, 44BL, 44BR, 79L, 79C, 79R, 80TL, 80TC, 80TR, 80BC, 80BR, 81TL, 81BL, 81BC, 81BR, 82L, 83TR, 83BL, 84TR, 90BL, 91L, 92TR, 93TL, 94R, 96C — Siebenthaler Nurseries: 56 — Soper, Dr. J.H.: 9BR — Stokes Seed Co.: 63.

Table of Contents

SHRUBS

SHRUBS

Ornamental shrubs add beauty and character to the garden

When we surround our homes with colorful gardens, graceful trees and shrubs, one of our aims is to make the house and other buildings appear dignified, attractive and of long standing. By correct landscaping, the choice of trees, evergreens and shrubs, we can even give a newly built home this effect.

Ornamental shrubs wisely selected and sited adds to the beauty and character of our gardens. They are the salvation for the new garden or the quick rejuvenation of a neglected one. Most shrubs reach maturity four or five years after planting, so there is not the long wait for results experienced with most shade trees.

The home gardener or landscape architect uses shrubs to blend the trees and the rest of the garden. Most shrubs are long lived and are almost as permanent as shade trees. This means that any money you spend on them can be considered a very stable investment.

The majority of ornamental shrubs are less expensive than trees or evergreens. This is a tremendous advantage for new home owners because they can achieve garden beauty quickly and at very little cost.

Shrubs can be used in many ways in our gardens. They are extremely effective when planted in borders composed almost entirely of shrubs and give rich background color in mixed borders for the brightly colored annuals, perennials, biennials and the various Spring, Summer and Fall flowering bulbs. In the mixed border they would be planted in groups throughout the entire length of the border.

They are very useful when sited as a screen, to give privacy or protection from the prevailing winds.

The foundation planting will be that much more colorful and lovely if it contains a large percentage of the dwarf ornamental shrubs.

Few people think of flowering shrubs in terms of the cut flower garden. The wise home gardener will plant several bushes of the easy-to-flower kinds like forsythia and flowering almond in a special cutting garden or in an out-of-the-way place to provide an adequate supply of branches for Winter forcing indoors.

The beauty and character of the garden can be varied considerably from month to month by choosing a group of shrubs which will provide a succession of flowers, berries or colorful foliage from early Spring until late Fall. The use of shrubs is not confined to the normal gardening season, because there is still another group having colorful bark which helps to brighten the winter landscape by providing a contrast from the evergreens in the foundation planting and other parts of the garden.

It is also possible to select shrubs whose foliage varies in color from silver through yellow, light and dark green to red.

There is another large section of ornamental shrubs which will help to attract many birds to the garden throughout the whole year.

Many of the ornamental shrubs, particularly the non-flowering types, are used as hedges — both high and low. In choosing shrubs for this purpose, be sure to pick those that have short, fibrous roots which will not overrun the rest of the garden and rob the lawn and flower beds of precious plant food and moisture.

A Rose of Sharon blooms when few other shrubs do

Nature and this is particularly true in preparing the soil for shrubs.

In poor soils, and unfortunately this is the case on most new subdivisions, we have to dig in humus at the rate of at least 8 to 10 bushels per 100 square feet. For those persons who are fortunate enough to have garden soils which are in reasonable condition, six bushels per 100 square feet would be sufficient.

In choosing the type of humus to use, the most important thing to keep in mind is the cost and how easily it is available. Any one of the following kinds of humus or organic matter will prove satisfactory: materials processed from sewage, peat moss, well-rotted barnyard manure, discarded mushroom manure, or material from the home compost heap.

As with any other part of the garden, you cannot grow things well with humus alone. Despite popular opinion, all forms of humus contain little or no plant foods. Well-rotted barnyard manure is supposed to contain quantities of plant food materials, but this is not true. Twenty- four hours after it is fresh it has lost 90% of its plant food value. To all intents and purposes, you can say that any form of humus you use does not contain any worthwhile amount of plant foods.

It is therefore essential to use a combination of complete fertilizer and humus. A complete fertilizer contains balanced amounts of nitrogen, phosphorus and potash and minor plant food elements necessary to good growth. At the same time as you work in the humus, be sure to add a complete fertilizer at the rate of 4 pounds per 100 square feet. The fertilizer, humus and soil should be thoroughly mixed together, down to a depth of 8 to 10 inches.

In making a selection of ornamental shrubs for *any* purpose, it is important to have the following information:

1. To what height will the shrub grow at maturity?
2. How wide will it be at maturity?
3. When does it flower?
4. What color are the flowers?
5. What color is the foliage?
6. Does it produce attractive berries?
7. Are the leaves colorful in the Fall?
8. Does it need full sun, or will it stand some shade?

Planting and care of shrubs

Preparation of the soil — It is a good plan to prepare the soil a week to ten days in advance of receiving the stock. If you observe shrubs growing out in nature, say along a hedge row or in the woods, and you examine the soil in which they are growing, you will discover that in nine cases out of ten they are growing in soil containing plenty of humus or organic matter. We never go wrong if we try to imitate Mother

The potentilla is almost as permanent as a shade tree

One of the biggest mistakes the beginner to gardening usually makes is to carry out the practise of pocket planting. By this we mean he digs a planting hole 2 feet square and 2 feet deep in either heavy or very light soils, he replaces the soil removed with a suitable soil mixture and proceeds to set the shrubs in place. When the roots start to grow, they gradually use up all the value contained in the special soil mixture and as they grow further, they run into the very poor soil surrounding the original planting hole. To avoid this, the best thing to do is to replace **all** the poor soil in the bed in the beginning with a first-class soil mixture.

Size to plant — The size of shrubs to plant would depend to some extent on whether you want an immediate effect, or are prepared to wait a year or two for results. In most cases, it is best to be a little patient and plant small, vigorous shrubs, 2 to 3 feet high. At this stage of growth they will recover quickly and look their best two or three years later. The bareness of such plantings can be alleviated easily and quickly by filling the beds and borders with a combination of colorful annuals, biennials, perennials and Spring, Summer and Fall flowering bulbs.

However, where an immediate effect is needed, the larger nurseries or garden centers frequently sell 4 to 5 foot specimens which are purchased with a ball of earth around them and burlapped, exactly like evergreens. Of course, these would be considerably more expensive.

Nurseries and garden centers now sell shrubs, roses and other plants in two ways; bare root, or in containers which can be planted at any time during the growing season. Which is best? There is little doubt that those you set out in the garden from containers are by far the best. There is almost no mortality and the plants do not receive any shock whatsoever.

On the other hand, many of the easy-to-grow shrubs like forsythias can be bought less expensively in a bare root condition, and if planted correctly, there is little chance of them not growing.

The best advice that can be given on planting is to prepare the planting holes before the nursery stock arrives, and set the shrubs just as soon as they are received.

Heeling in — In some instances there may be reasons why the shrubs and other plants can not be immediately set in the ground. In this event, do not allow the plants to languish in the garage or basement for several days as the roots and bark will dry out. The best thing to do is what the nurseryman calls "heeling in."

Trenches 8 to 10 inches deep should be dug, one side of which will be vertical, and the other sloping upwards from the bottom of the hole at a 45° angle. Next, the bundles of shrubs should be opened, the roots spread out in the bottom of the trench, and covered with moist earth. Make sure the soil is firmed well around the roots to eliminate any air pockets. Provided that the earth is not allowed to dry out at any time, nursery stock will stay in good planting shape for 10 to 14 days when treated this way.

Root puddling — The biggest single reason why shrubs and most other nursery stock die after planting, is almost invariably the result of poor planting methods. In all too many cases a shipment of nursery stock will arrive and be left around for the weekend or even longer before planting. Usually it is left in the garage and very often the garage door will be left open with the roots at the mercy of the wind and the sun.

In still other cases the nursery stock will be taken from the package at planting time and left exposed during planting operations.

The best method of transplanting nursery stock is the one universally used by commercial nurserymen. It is called "root puddling". By following this method the various shrubs and trees are almost certain to grow. This is where you can call in the help of any children in your family, because it is almost comparable to making mud pies.

First of all you make up a heavy batter of ordinary soil and water of a very thick consistency. Be sure to give the soil and water a good stirring until it is very evenly and thoroughly mixed. You can make doubly sure of good results by making up a solution consisting of one gallon of water and two teaspoons of a liquid fertilizer. Use this solution to mix with the earth in place of plain water. It will give your plants a quicker start and an extra reserve of energy.

Swish the roots around in the batter and .

The Japanese Quince provides early Springtime beauty

Forsythia is one of the first shrubs to bloom in Spring

when thoroughly soaked, remove them and sprinkle the wet roots with some good fine earth. For this purpose, the best thing to use is one of the commercially prepared soil mixtures, such as the one sold for African violets. This will provide a protective coating over the fine root hairs and will just about guarantee a successful transplanting.

How to plant — All bare rooted shrubs should be given a good soaking before planting. This will not be necessary if you follow the root puddling plan mentioned before. If the shrubs are in containers these should be given a thorough soaking, 2 or 3 hours at least, before planting is to take place. Actually, the best system is to give them a good soaking the night before so that they will be ready for planting the next morning. When shrubs planted in containers are treated in this manner, the root ball comes easily from the container and very little if any earth surrounding the roots will drop away.

In the case of bare-rooted shrubs, all dried and damaged roots should be cut cleanly and the branches thinned and cut back to one-third before they are planted. In doing this pruning, we must keep in mind the natural form or shape of the shrub.

A planting hole should be dug that is large enough and deep enough to allow the roots to spread out naturally, and not be cramped in the slightest way. This generally means that the hole will have to be two feet square and two feet deep. The soil removed should be replaced with a prepared top soil mixture. Again, the one you buy for use in root puddling would be ideal. Such soil mixtures are available from almost any nursery or garden store selling garden supplies.

Sufficient soil mixture should be placed in the bottom of the hole so that the shrub will be two or three inches deeper than it

grew in the nursery. In the center of the hole the soil should be raised up in a two inch mound on which to set the shrub.

This will eliminate the possibility of an air pocket developing in the bottom of the planting hole.

Next, work the soil among the roots and then add another two or three inches, firming well as you add it. Keep adding soil and firming until the hole is half full. Then get out the hose and fill the remainder of the hole with water. Let this drain away completely before filling in the remainder of the hole with soil mixture.

Where the shrubs are to be planted out of containers you will not have to set them as deep as those with bare roots. The top of the soil of the container-grown plants should be set just one inch below the surface of the surrounding soil.

Again, we must be careful to firm the soil around the edges of the ball of earth covering the roots so that the air pockets are completely eliminated. It is not necessary to add water as you do in planting the bare root shrubs.

Immediately after planting it is good practise to put down a mulch of humus or organic matter two to three inches deep which should extend out from the trunk,

A charming scene

A flowering crab apple

9

well beyond the outer spread of the branches. This will go a long way to help keep the roots cool, and preserve the supply of moisture in the soil. It will also practically eliminate the need for cultivation.

Watering—It is very important the first year to keep the newly planted shrubs moist at all times. This does not mean that you get out the hose and give them a light sprinkling every day, because this will do more harm than good. It will encourage the development of surface roots and will give fungus diseases such as powdery mildew the right conditions in which to develop and spread. The best plan is to water once a week making sure the moisture penetrates the earth to a depth of 6 to 8 inches.

The best way of accomplishing this is to use one of the plastic or canvas soakers which lets the water ooze out gently at a rate which the soil can absorb. It also makes sure the water touches only the soil and not the foliage as would happen by using the hose or a sprinkler system.
Frequent spraying of the leaves produces exactly the right conditions for the development and eventual spreading of the various fungus diseases.

These are the general rules for watering but it must be realized that they may need varying to suit different locations. For instance a foundation planting or border which faces south might require a good soaking more often than one facing north or in the shade of a building. You will learn by experience what is needed for your own garden.

Feeding—Provided that the shrubs have been planted in a good soil at the beginning, no further feeding will be needed during the first season after planting. From then on, they should be fed once a year in the early

Spring. The most satisfactory time would be in April, just as soon as the soil becomes workable. The amount of fertilizer to use can be figured out on the basis of four pounds per 100 square feet of bed or border area, or a large handful for individual bushes. Scatter the fertilizer around each shrub, just beyond the outer spread of the branches. This is where the feeder roots are located and they will be able to absorb the plant foods dissolved in the soil moisture and then transfer them to the leaves.

After applying, the fertilizer should be gently worked into the soil with a rake or hoe. For this purpose we use a complete fertilizer containing balanced amounts of nitrogen, phosphorus and potash. It is most important that the fertilizer you use does not contain a high percentage of nitrogen, compared to the phosphorus and potash. Too much nitrogen causes the shrubs to produce a lot of green vegetative growth, with very few flowers.

Again, these are the general ground rules for fertilizing. You may find that if your soils are the very light sandy type the shrubs will have to be fed two or three times a season rather than just the once. As we pointed out in previous books, the particles of soil in the sandy type are extremely large when compared to those of the heavy clay.

Keep newly planted shrubs moist

Pruning depends on flowering time

Every time it rains or you water the bed or border, some of the plant food in the soil dissolves in this moisture and leaches or drains away, instead of being soaked up by the humus. This means that far more fertilizer will be required in the sandy soils than in the heavy clay.

Pruning — No one should attempt pruning unless they have good tools for the job. These would include:

1. A pair of hand pruners or secaturs for small cuts not over $\frac{1}{4}$ inch in diameter. Best kind for this purpose are those having a steel blade which cuts against a brass plate. Both the blades and the brass plates are replaceable.
2. A pair of long-handled pruners for larger cuts measuring up to $1\frac{1}{4}$ inch in diameter. These have tubular steel handles and shock absorbing rubber grips.
3. A small jig-saw for use in spots where it is not possible to get an ordinary pruning saw.
4. A pruning saw with a blade about 14 inches long and not more than 1 inch to 2 inches wide. It is possible to buy such saws having a blade which folds back into the handle when not in use.

Purpose of pruning—The real reason for pruning shrubs is to keep them young, and if done regularly from the time the shrubs are first planted, it will require little time or labour on your part. Pruning only becomes a big chore and a job for the expert when it is neglected for a number of years.

The correct procedure once the shrubs are well established is to remove a few of the oldest shoots each year. This means that you would be removing those which are 3 or 4 years only. Such a method will encourage the development of strong new shoots from the base of the plant.

A time to prune — Unfortunately, it is impossible to say that there is a special time for pruning shrubs, because this depends on when they bloom. Hydrangea and the butterfly bush are typical examples of a group of shrubs which flower in the late Spring or Summer. These and all members of their class have to be pruned in late Winter or in very early Spring. In this group are:

Hibiscus (Rose of Sharon)
Buddleia (Butterfly Bush)
Abelia
Kerria
Hydrangea
Honeysuckles
Hybrid Tea Roses
Late flowering Tamarix

Early Spring flowering shrubs, notably forsythia, are pruned after the flowering period is over, just as you would climbing roses. It is a mistake to prune this type of shrub in the late Winter, because there is the chance you may remove branches which should provide the annual Spring display of bloom.

The following are typical examples of this group:

Cydonia (Flowering Quince)
Deutzia
Forsythia (Golden Bells)
Climbing roses
Magnolia Stellata
Lilacs
Most Viburnums
Alpine Currant
Spiraeas
Shrub roses
Coralberry
Weigelia

A common mistake in pruning which is not only confined to beginners is to take a pair of pruners and give their shrubs a trimming similar to a crew cut. In other words, they shorten each branch to the same length, causing a few fuzzy places of foliage at the top and bare branches underneath. This type of treatment will eliminate most of the flowers, and what is more important, will surely and effectively destroy the graceful shape of the shrub. The only time this manner of pruning should be used is when trimming hedges as in this case we are con-

cerned with creating a bright green symmetrical wall. We said earlier that when pruning we aim to keep the shrub young, graceful and full of bloom. In practise this is accomplished by cutting out a few of the oldest shoots each year. Once the shrubs have become well established it means removing those that are 3 to 4 years old. Be ruthless and remove these shoots right down to the ground, taking care not to leave a series of stubs 2 to 4 inches in length or even longer. Such stubs offer an open invitation to insects and diseases to attack the bushes. In particular they form an easy access for borers. When a shrub or tree is attacked by the borer, it is finished, the only recourse being to remove the tree or shrub and plant new or healthy stock.

Control of insects and diseases

This is not a difficult problem but to get satisfactory results you should use two methods.

First, before growth starts and when the temperature is above 40°, forestall the attacks of scale insects by spraying with a dormant oil spray. Most of the larger chemical companies package a dormant oil spray for the home gardener and its application is neither difficult nor expensive.

Secondly, as soon as the leaves appear, spray or dust your shrubs with an all-purpose fungicide and insecticide. Spraying should take place at least once every 10 days but preferably every week. If a heavy rainstorm occurs soon after the dusting or spraying it will pay to repeat, as most of the effect of the spray or the dust will be lost during the rainfall. This means that in most areas the spraying or dusting program would last from some time in May until September.

Most popular flowering shrubs

BUDDLEIA or Butterfly Bush (4 to 6 feet). As an ornamental lawn shrub and a Summer cut flower the **buddleia** or butterfly bush is in a class by itself. It is unsurpassed in beauty and usefulness for gardens large or small. From July until frost it produces an abundance of rich, dazzling panicles of bloom that demand instant attention. Each of these can measure from 6 to 14 inches in length. Butterfly bush is the com-

The Buddleia is unsurpassed as an ornamental lawn shrub

The Buddleia is called the butterfly bush because it is attractive to butterflies

mon name of this attractive shrub and it receives its name because it attracts butterflies to the garden in great numbers. The plants grow 4 to 6 feet high and the foliage is a deep leathery green. The rich colors of the flowers are greatly intensified under artificial light and they harmonize well in all types of flower arrangements.

Provided you buy quality stock, you should get bloom the first year.

Home gardeners who already have some bushes in their garden will discover that to get maximum bloom every year they have to prune their bushes down to within one foot of the ground each year in the late Winter or early Spring.

It will be realized that this heavy pruning is severe when compared to pruning any other shrub, but nevertheless this is the type of pruning that forces the bushes to give masses of top quality bloom. A buddleia is like a hybrid tea rose, and flowers on the new wood produced each Spring.

For maximum bloom in the colder districts the buddleia bushes require some Winter protection. You have to cover the crown of the plant with several shovelsful of earth each Fall before the ground is frozen solid. You might say it is exactly the same kind of Winter protection as you would give hybrid tea and floribunda roses.

Recommended Varieties:

Blue Wonder — Long sprays, beautiful blue.

Burgundy — Large sprays, 2 feet in length of a rich dark, royal purple.

Dubonnet — Dark wine.

Fascinating—Soft orchid pink.

Ile De France—Violet purple, and very fragrant.

Peace—Pure white.

Royal Red—Deep reddish purple.

Empire Blue—Finest blue.

Fortune—Lilac sprays 12 to 18 inches in length.

Charming—Deep pink.

CYDONIA or Flowering Quince (5 to 6 feet) — The flowering quince is another fine addition to the list of flowering shrubs for the garden. In the early Spring the bushes are covered with the most brilliant red or rose-pink flowers, long before most of the other shrubs have started to blossom.

The dazzling eye-catching flowers cover the branches from the ground up. Branches of the flowering quince are wonderful for cutting. The bushes will grow as much as five or six feet in height, however, they can be kept much lower by pruning. They can also be trained like a grape vine to cover a wall or trellis, Side pruning is not necessary, but you must prune out the dead wood each year immediately after flowering.

Recommended Varieties:

Charming — Large flowers of soft salmon pink.

Coral Beauty—Coral red blooms.

Falconet Charlot —Double salmon-pink flowers.

Hollandia—Enormous bunches of scarlet red, wide open flowers 1½ inches across.

Nivalis—Best pure white.

Rowallane — Rich vermillion red blooms.

Stanford Red—Blooms open geranium red and deepen to an intense blood red.

Crimson Gold — Bright red blossoms with gold center.

COTINUS (Smoke Tree or Rhus) (7 feet)—Here is a fine flowering shrub which has the added advantage of having attractive foliage as well. Plants have a neat compact habit of growth and make excellent lawn specimen trees. The cut branches are very useful as fillers for bouquets, especially with chrysanthemums.

Flowering quince bushes grow 5 to 6 feet high

Charming deep pink Buddleia

Recommended Varieties:

Royal Purple — Foliage is a magnificent rich dark purple which lasts throughout the entire growing season from approximately the 1st of May until late Fall. Large red feathery plumes appear on the bushes during July and cover the entire bush. Royal Purple is a marvellous variety for screens or backgrounds.

Purple Fringe—A most attractive variety whose purple flowers form clouds of smoke-like bloom which seem to float gracefully on its stems. Like the varieties of smoke trees it makes an exceptional lawn specimen shrub.

DEUTZIA (2 to 4 feet)—The deutzias comprise a group of showy flowering shrubs which originally came to our gardens from Asia. Their attractive flowers are produced in early Summer, with most of them being white in color, but some have a pinkish tinge. In the colder areas, where the temperature falls below zero consistently in the Winter they will need a protected spot in the garden.

The bushes produce many stems which rise up directly from the root, curving upward and outward. The foliage almost completely disappears under the tremendous panicles of small, frilled, bell-like flowers. The recommended varieties listed below will be welcomed in many gardens because they bloom quite well even in fairly heavy shade.

Gracilis — One of the prettiest and the most graceful of all the deutzias. Gracilis will flower better in the shade than almost any other flowering shrub. Bushes average 2 to 3 feet in height and are attractive at all times of the year. In late May and early June they are covered with an astonishing profusion of elegant snow-white flowers. This variety is particularly useful for edgings to walks or paths and for planting in clumps in the foreground of the foundation bed or border.

Kalmiae Flora — Do not let the rather difficult name deter you from planting this loveliest of shrubs. The bushes are low-growing, with slightly arching slender branches. They are covered in late May and early June with eye-catching pink flowers. Bushes will not grow over 3 feet in height making it an excellent shrub for the small garden.

DAPHNE (1 to 5 feet)—For the front of the foundation planting you will not go wrong if you plant the fragrant and very delightful daphne. It is a shrub which is spreading in habit, reaches about 18 inches in width and 10 to 12 inches high at maturity. Bright pink, and fragrant flowers cover the bushes in the very early Spring and again in the late Fall.

Large pockets in the rock garden, along walks or driveways and in groups in front of the mixed or shrub border are other worthwhile spots to plant the daphne.

This dwarf shrub is also well liked because its foliage is evergreen and persists throughout the Winter. It is extremely hardy and will survive in all but the very coldest parts.

Daphne needs to be planted in a sunny location where the soil is well-drained.

Branches of the flowering quince are used indoors

14

Deutzias bloom in late Spring

The fragrant garland flower

Recommended Varieties:

Cneorum—also called Garland Flower. This variety has a spreading habit and grows from 8 to 12 inches tall. It produces delicately perfumed rose-pink blossoms.

Somerset — Here we have a variety which originated in England.

During May and early June plants are covered with delightfully scented, blush pink star-shaped flowers in clusters 6 to 8 inches long. Somerset will grow and flower exceptionally well in light shade. The foliage is dark green, giving the plants the appearance of boxwood. If left unclipped it will grow about 5 feet high and four feet wide.

Genkwa (Lilac daphne) — One of the finest gems of the garden for the very early Spring. Depending on the season and location, it starts to flower in March and continues into April. Lilac-like blue flowers are produced on graceful branches before the foliage appears. Bushes eventually will reach 3 feet in height and are fine for growing in the flower border, rock garden or towards the back of the shrub border. Likes well-drained ordinary garden soil, and will thrive without protection in localities where the temperatures fall to below zero.

FORSYTHIA (Golden Bells) (6 to 8 feet)—It has often been said that there is no such thing as a bargain in the gardening world. By that, it is meant that there is no point in buying plants, bulbs or other nursery stock which sell for ridiculously low prices. Just the same, there are some bargains to be had by planting in our gardens a shrub that serves two purposes. The various forsythias will do just that.

In warmer parts, Daphne will keep its evergreen foliage from year to year

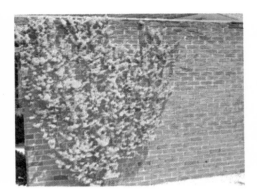

Forsythias climb up the wall

In March, April and May, depending on where you live, they provide the garden with masses of bright yellow blossoms which are always particularly welcome after a long, hard winter. These same branches, gathered after the first of January and placed in water in a warm room will flower equally as well indoors.

About the only problem that occurs in cutting branches for indoor flowering is that you reduce the Spring show of bloom. Some of you may say "That is all right with me, I prefer the bloom during the Winter months when no other is available". However, the answer really lies in planting some extra bushes in an out of the way spot, such as the vegetable or cutting garden which would only be used for forcing. You would then be able to cut away to your

Deutzias originated in Asia

heart's content, without harming the Spring display in the foundation planting or shrub border.

Recommended Varieties:

Beatrix Farrand is a beautiful new forsythia which originated in the Arnold Arboretum in Boston and was named for Beatrix Farrand, one of North America's foremost women landscape architects. It is a vigorous variety and makes a large symmetrical bush which reaches 6 to 8 feet tall at maturity. Flowers are a really deep golden yellow, and are immense in size, averaging 1½ inches across. Some of the blossoms grow to an unbelievable 2 inches in diameter. Branches are smothered with flowers to their very tips.

Lynnwood Gold — A new forsythia from Ireland which seems likely to become the leading deep yellow kind. Branches are

The Smoke bush or cotinus has attractive foliage

16

Forsythia grows 6 to 8 feet tall at maturity

Spring Glory will guarantee a sparkling and cheerful display in your garden early next Spring at a time when no other shrub will be in flower. The pale yellow blossoms are equally attractive and delightful whether flowering in the Spring garden, or used to make Spring come two or three months ahead of time in the home.

Suspensa — A magnificent drooping form of forsythia which originated in Japan. It is a low-growing, vigorous spreading shrub, invaluable for placing high on a bank or at the top of a retaining wall from which it will trail down in an exquisite yellow stream. Other choice spots to plant Suspensa would be in groups at the front of the border, or as an attractive ground cover on a sloping bank.

HIBISCUS (Rose of Sharon or Althea) (8 to 10 feet) — The hardy types of the hibiscus are tall and upright in growth and have a fine rounded form. We prize them highly in the home garden because of their colorful flowers and their late flowering season which starts in July and lasts until frost. This is a time of the year when there will be few other flowering shrubs in bloom. They are not a bit particular about the kind of soil in which they are planted, except that it must be well-drained. Make no mistake, they require full sun to grow well.

erect and are completely covered with golden yellow flowers. **Individual** blooms are of better substance and do not seem to mind the bad weather we often get in the early Spring. It is a variety that is absolutely superb for cutting and forcing into flower in the house during the Winter months. At maturity it will be 5 to 7 feet high, depending on the soil conditions and makes an ideal companion for the pale yellow Spring Glory.

Spring Glory—Talk to many home gardeners and they will tell you that Spring Glory would be their choice, if they could choose only one type of forsythia for their garden. Once you have seen this loveliest of all the golden bells in flower, you will not be able to forget the picture for a long time to come. The branches are erect but so much bloom is produced that they actually bend with the weight. Several bushes of

Deutzias flower reasonably well in heavy shade

Plant extra bushes in the cutting garden for forcing purposes

until frost. Most white hibiscus blooms do not fully open, and are therefore not showy. Rev. W. Smith is the exception, and its flowers are large open, wide and are best described as superb.

Hamabo — A very colorful Rose of Sharon. Flowers are a brilliant combination of red and white, and contrast beautifully **with** the dark green foliage.

HYDRANGEA (Paniculata Grandiflora —Pee Gee) (6 to 8 feet)—It is always difficult to find a shrub which will flower

Very little pruning is required for these colorful shrubs, neither do they require any spraying.

Most beginners to gardening think that their Roses of Sharon have not survived the first Winter because the foliage does not appear on the branches until very late in the Spring, but it must be remembered this is probably one of the latest shrubs to show foliage in the Spring.

Recommended Varieties:

Celestial Blue — A magnificent distinct and truly blue Rose of Sharon. The gorgeous single disc-like blue flowers are produced in quantities. Planted with a white variety, it will create an eye-catching color effect from July until frost.

Woodbridge — Produces very large, wide open flaring flowers whose color is a clear rose pink. This is the best and most brilliant of the pink Roses of Sharon.

Rev. W. Smith — Large, pure white flowers are produced which open flat and appear in great numbers from early July

Spring Glory is a lovely forsythia

The Rose of Sharon is one of the latest shrubs to bloom in Spring

Pee Gee hydrangea

Spring, because the new bloom will be produced on the current year's wood. In the case of the tree form, you would cut back each branch to within 3 inches of the crown at the top of the stem.

Hydrangea Arborescens (Hills of Snow) (3 feet)—Here is the ideal shrub for a shady spot. The low compact 3 foot plants are covered with massive, pure white, snowball-like blooms from July to September. Foliage is a lush, deep green and the leaves have an attractive heart shape. Its

in late Summer, if you require this, many persons overlook the Pee Gee hydrangea. This extremely attractive shrub will grow well in the sun, in partial shade, or even on the north side of a house. In August, immense cone-shaped heads of bloom start to appear and these remain in flower until the end of October. In the beginning they open up a creamy white in color, and then gradually change to a fascinating shade of pink. When hit by the first heavy frosts in late October or early November, they change to a fine bronze shade.

The Pee Gee hydrangea is hardy practically anywhere. It can be easily grown either in a shrub form, or in a standard or tree form, similar to a rose. Be sure and specify which type you want when you order from your favorite nursery or garden center. The flowers are excellent for cutting and will last for a long time.

The tree or standard form of the Pee Gee hydrangea grows to a maximum height of 6 feet and of course has the same flowers as the shrub type.

Both the shrub and the standard forms can be pruned back severely in the early

Very little pruning is required for Rose of Sharon

19

biggest asset is its ability to thrive in varied conditions of shade or full sun. The Hills of Snow hydrangea makes a fine lawn specimen shrub and is equally beautiful at the front of border plantings. To secure large blooms, cut back to within 4 to 6 inches of the ground each Spring. The flowers are produced on the current year's wood, just like hybrid tea roses.

KOLKWITZIA (Beauty Bush) (6 to 7 feet)—The kolkwitzia is known as the shrub of a thousand flowers. It is doubtful if any other flowering plant bears so many flowers and provides the garden with such a show of color each June and July. It originally came from China, and its gracefulness, free blooming quality and hardiness makes it worthy of an important place in any garden.

The center branches of the beauty bush grow upright to a maximum height of seven feet, while the outer branches arch out and downwards to the ground. They bear clusters of deep pink bell-shaped flowers with yellowish-brown throats.

The beauty bush grows very well even in the poorest soils and needs very little pruning. The bushes seem to shape them-

Pure white flower of a superb Rose of Sharon

selves and are never thin or bare at the bottom. There is never any problem about its hardiness.

LABURNUM (Golden Chain Tree) (8 to 10 feet)—This is one of our dual-purpose garden plants which can be grown either as a shrub or a tree. The long clustered golden chain or laburnum produces flowers which are not unlike those of the wisteria and are a beautiful golden yellow in color. Flowering time is June, and the hanging clusters measure 18 to 20 inches in length. It is not only extremely beautiful when in bloom, but is most colorful during the rest of the garden season. Both the bark and foliage are attractive. The laburnum is best planted in some shade or

Hydrangea Hortensis is the familiar gift plant

Laburnum is to be planted in shade

on the north side of a house. It will grow extremely well when planted among other tall shrubs.

It will usually flower the first year after planting. As it is not hardy in the colder areas, check with your local nursery man, garden club or horticultural society before you plant.

The beauty bush grows and flowers well even in poor soils

The shrub of a thousand flowers

Laburnums flower in late June

LILACS

The lilac is one of the best loved shrubs in all of North America. Most people look forward to "lilac time" in May and June when tremendous bursts of bloom fill the garden with color and fragrance.

When is the best time to plant lilacs? In the colder areas they can only be planted in the Spring, but where milder weather prevails, Fall planting is the most satisfactory because lilacs planted at that time will usually flower a year ahead of those planted the previous Spring. However, do not expect lilacs to flower correctly with full size flowers until at least two years

after planting.

It is most important to select a sunny location in the garden where there is good air circulation.

Under no circumstances will lilacs tolerate shade. They are not too fussy about the type of soil in which they are planted except that the lightest and the heaviest kinds should contain extra humus.

Before planting, be sure and work into the soil a quantity of both humus and complete fertilizer. Any of the following forms of humus can be used with success: materials processed from sewage, peat moss, well-rotted barnyard manure, discarded mushroom manure or material from the home compost heap. For ordinary garden soils

apply the chosen humus at the rate of 6 bushels per hundred square feet. In poor soils, either heavy or light, 10 bushels per 100 square feet will not be too much.

The complete fertilizer is applied at the rate of 4 pounds per 100 square feet.

The best type of lilac plant to buy is one that is well branched and 2 to 3 feet in height. Do not be persuaded to buy single stem plants. Make sure that you purchase your lilacs from a reliable nursery or garden center who sell "lilacs grafted on their own root stock", rather than those grafted on common lilac or privet stock.

Just before planting, prune out broken or dried out roots. In doing the actual planting operation, keep in mind that too deep

The Hills of Snow hydrangea is a magnificent shrub

Lilacs make excellent cut flowers

or too shallow planting is one of the most frequent causes of lilacs failing to flower or to produce large, top quality blooms. Dig the planting hole two feet deep, and two feet square. Loosen the earth in the bottom of the hole and then add a 10 inch layer of well-rotted barnyard manure or one of the other forms of humus mentioned before. On top of this place enough top soil so that the lilac plant will be 3 inches lower than the original planting in the nursery. This can be recognized by the distinct soil line on the trunk of the bush.

Spread the roots of the lilac bush to all sides of the hole, then add 3 to 4 inches of a mixture of two parts top soil and one part humus. Experienced home gardeners will be able to make up their own mixture, but for the beginner, it is usually best to buy one of the commercially prepared mixtures. Firm the soil around the roots so that air pockets are completely eliminated. Then fill the planting hole with water and let it drain completely away before filling in the remainder of the hole. This helps to settle the soil around the roots and just about guarantees the elimination of any air pockets.

Crape myrtle trees

Fall planted lilacs will need a coarse mulch of hay, straw or well-rotted barn-yard manure to keep the frost from heaving them out of the ground. To be effective, this should be 3 to 4 inches deep.

Lilacs that fail to bloom

Every Spring many home gardeners discover that their lilacs have failed to bloom. The causes of this are rather difficult to discover, because there are many reasons for non-flowering.

Regular pruning is probably the number one cause of a lilac failing to bloom. The flower buds on this finest of Spring flowering shrub are developed two seasons before and so the regular and liberal use of pruning shears cannot help but remove these buds. Lilacs should only be pruned enough to keep the plants in shape. Avoid planting lilacs in locations where it is necessary to restrict their height, as the constant pruning will prevent their blooming. It is far better in this type of location to use other low-growing shrubs.

The time to prune lilacs is immediately after they have finished flowering. One of

Lilacs start to bloom the end of May

Clark's Giant lilacs

24

Lilacs need a lot of sunshine

Frequently lilacs will get out of hand and reach lofty heights around the house. In such cases it is advisable to remove only half the wood at a time, leaving the rest to be cut back three or four seasons later when the new growth has had time to set buds.

As we mentioned earlier, lilacs need a fairly rich soil; in addition to this they also require plenty of lime to enable them to grow well. Where you have some bushes which have failed to bloom, a peck of ground agricultural limestone worked into the soil beneath the branches just as soon as the soil is workable in the Spring, will often do wonders towards getting the bushes to bloom again.

No lilac will flower unless it gets at least six hours of full uninterrupted sunshine each day. There is no truth to the idea that there are male and female lilacs and that one of each is necessary for flowering. Lilacs are like most flowering plants, having both male and female parts in the same flower.

Very often a lilac can be made to bloom again by giving it a good root pruning. Dig a trench 2 feet deep just inside the drip line of the branches and prune away all the roots that extend beyond the trench. In the soil removed from the trench, you mix a generous amount of super phosphate, (about 8 ounces to every three feet of trench) and then return the soil. This root pruning seems to shock the plants into flowering once again, not only for the one season, but for several years to come.

Insect and disease problems

Borers — Diseased and neglected lilacs are often attacked by borers. These attacks are easily recognized because the leaves begin to get small and discolored, and the branches start to droop and break. Around the first of August is the time to examine your lilac bushes for borers. When inspecting the plants, pay particular attention to the base looking for sawdust and spots wetted by sap which usually appears on infected plants. Borers are difficult to control in any plant and those attacking lilacs are no exception. In most cases about the only thing you can do is to discard the affected bushes and replant.

Oyster Shell Scale—Oyster shell scale is often a pest on many lilac bushes. The rough, gray infestations resembling small scales are easily visible on the stems and

the main things to guard against is letting the bushes become too thick or too dense. This happens when too many suckers or branches spring up from the base of the lilacs forcing the bushes to grow too high consequently they develop less and less flowers. The best plan to control suckers is to cut out all but three or four of them per bush with sharp pruners. At the same time also cut out any dead or diseased wood.

Next, cut out 3 or 4 of the older branches to provide more space for the younger ones to grow and at the same time give the center of the bush some much needed light and air circulation.

It is important to know whether you have the ordinary Persian lilac or the French hybrids. The suckers of Persian lilacs will eventually grow so thickly, the bush will

stop flowering and will become almost a jungle. However, if all but three or four of them are removed, those remaining will eventually produce a flowering branch.

The same thing happens with French hybrids if the bushes are grafted on their own roots. On the other hand, when grafted on privet stock, which is usually the case, any suckers that do come up will not produce flowering branches but stems of a privet bush. Naturally, these should be removed as they appear or your lilac bush will gradually revert to a privet.

It is important to remove the old flower heads after the flowers have faded. We do this to prevent the formation of unsightly seed heads and to stop the energy of the plant from being used in producing seeds instead of the following year's flowering buds.

25

branches. Scale is best controlled by regular spraying or dusting with an insecticide when insects are active in early Summer.

Powdery mildew—About the only fungus disease to attack lilacs is powdery mildew. In the case of the lilacs, it is really a harmless fungus disease but one which can be very unsightly and wide-spread in the late Summer and Fall. Mildew can be kept under almost complete control by dusting or spraying every 3 weeks with an all-round fungicide.

Recommended Varieties:

About 40 years ago a U.S. nurseryman, the late W. B. Clark, decided that something should be done to improve the quality and color range of lilacs. He imported all the varieties he could find, and crossed them with domestic types. The results set a new standard for size, color and quality of the lilac flowers.

Clark's Giant was the first of this new group of lilacs. The single, soft gentian blue flowers average an enormous 1¼ to

Trees lawns and flowers beautify a garden

1½ inches across. They are borne in huge pyramidal-like clusters which can measure 12 inches long and 7 to 8 inches wide at the base. These are carried well above the foliage and have a wonderful, true lilac fragrance.

Esther Staley—Opinion has it that this **one** variety is the best pink lilac to date. It produces red buds which open into large single pink flowers without the usual lavender tinge. Clusters are of good size and are freely produced in mid-season. Bushes are healthy and have a remarkable vigor.

Pink Spray—Another delightful single pink. It blooms earlier than Esther Staley and is a somewhat softer shade. Its flowers have a daintiness and charm further enhanced by stamens that show prettily. As a cut flower, Pink Spray lasts unusually well.

Sweetheart — A desirable variety. The striking contrast between its deep, reddish-mauve buds and its double, palest lavender flowers is quite unusual. Clusters

A flowering shrub provides shade and beauty

An eye-catching magnolia takes your breath away

are of medium size, blooms are medium-large. Flowering time is mid-season.

Splendor—Extends the lilac season by blooming from mid to late Spring. Its dark, reddish-purple buds open into flowers of purplish-blue. These are large, double and well placed in clusters of good size. The bronzy hue of its new growth is an uncommon characteristic.

Primrose— It produces large double blooms a rich, creamy yellow in color. The bushes have all the good points of the French hybrid lilacs, and grow 8 to 10 feet tall. It is beautiful when used as a lawn specimen, or planted in the foundation bed or shrub border.

Nocturne — A lovely hardy variety which develops immense spikes of rich, blue flowers which measure up to 18 inches in length. Since this variety blooms later than the French hybrids, it materially extends the lilac season.

Standard French hybrids

Charles Joly—Double dark red.

Belle de Nancy—Double bright rose.

General Sheridan—Double white, late season.

Hugo Koster—Deep lilac-blue.

President Grevy — Clear soft delicate blue, semi-double to double.

Congo—Single deep purplish-red.

Edith Cavel—Double white.

Ellen Willmott—Double snow-white.

Katherine Haveneyer—Double cobalt blue.

Ludwig Spaeth—Single purple.

Madam Lemoine—Double pure white.

Marshall Foch — Single carmine rose, deep carmine in bud.

Massena—Large single deep purple-red.

Mrs. Edward Harding—Bright double purple-red.

Olivia de Serres — Double lavender-blue, purple in bud.

President Poincare — Double deep purple.

MAGNOLIA

There is nothing more eye-catching or breathtaking in the early Spring garden than a pink or white magnolia in full bloom. This fine flowering shrub has the advantage over other shrubs as its blooming period takes place at a time when few other shrubs or trees are in bloom.

Except in the southern part of the United States, the varieties of magnolias we grow in the home garden originally came from Asia.

Magnolias, although being slow growers, are very easy to handle in the garden. Their main requirement is to be planted in a rich soil that stays moderately moist. This means that humus at the minimum rate of six bushels per 100 square feet must be dug into the soil before planting. In very heavy clay soils, or light sandy ones, it is better to step this amount up to 8 to 10 bushels per 100 square feet.

At the same time, work into the soil a complete fertilizer at the rate of 4 pounds per 100 square feet.

The hardy magnolias are one of the few flowering shrubs that need to be transplanted *when in bloom*. This is necessary because the roots of this most colorful of shrubs are very tender and will not heal except when the bush is growing actively.

Once planted, very little care or maintenance is required. Growth is fairly slow and almost no pruning is needed. Magnolias

The saucer magnolia has huge cup-shaped pink flowers

The star magnolia has many-petalled blooms

do like to have the soil above their roots covered with a mulch at least 2 to 3 inches deep. This should extend out from the trunk, to well beyond the outer spread of the branches. Any of the commonly used forms of humus mentioned before in this book will be satisfactory for mulching purposes. A mulch will help keep the soil moist and the roots cool.

In colder areas, be sure to plant on the south or protected side of the home where there will be lots of warm, early Spring sunshine. If you live in the coldest districts, it is well to wrap the shrub with burlap for the Winter months.

Magnolias are always shipped with a ball of earth surrounding the roots in the same manner as evergreens. You do not remove the burlap from around the roots, as eventually this will rot away and become part of the soil.

Planting directions for magnolias are exactly the same as for evergreens.

Recommended Varieties:

Soulangeana (Saucer magnolia)—This variety produces a breathtaking beautiful display with its huge cup-shaped pink

28

flowers. These will average from 5 to 10 inches in diameter. The foliage is shiny and attractive. Plants grow to a maximum height of 20 feet, so it is a good idea to keep in mind when choosing a suitable location.

Alexandrina — Another fine variety of Soulangeana whose large white cup-shaped flowers have a purple-stained flesh at the base on the outside of the blooms. If anything, Alexandrina is earlier than the pink variety mentioned above.

Nigra — This variety has lovely lily-shaped flowers. The beautiful purple blooms are long and tapering and last for a much longer period than the pink and white types. Plants are compact, and the branches begin quite low.

Stellata (Star magnolia) — Produces many petalled, star-like blooms which appear very early in the Spring. The fragrant flowers appear before any of the leaves and as the buds unfold, the tree suddenly breaks forth into almost indescribable

Mock orange or philadelphus is easy to grow

The golden leaf mock orange

beauty. Star magnolias grow about 20 feet high, with a spread of 15 to 20 feet.

Doctor Merrill — A star-like magnolia which, unlike magnolia Stellata, grows rapidly and transplants without the slightest difficulty.

Early in the Spring, this new variety is covered with white star-like blossoms. It makes a fine lawn specimen tree because the foliage is excellent. Needs planting in full sun for best results and is as hardy as any oak tree.

MALUS (Flowering Crab Apples) — Each Spring the Japanese flowering cherries in Washington receive much deserved publicity. Unfortunately, they are not reliably hardy everywhere but we are lucky in having the flowering crab apples to take their place. Not only do they give our gardens a much better show of bloom, but at the same time they are extremely hardy.

Many persons would think crab apples are trees. This is very true, but actually they are what we call a dual-purpose plant,

29

which can be grown equally as well as a shrub, or tree, depending on the way they are pruned at the nursery. Be sure to specify which type you want when you place your order at the nursery or garden center.

They do not require any special type of soil, and will grow well in ordinary garden earth. The method of planting is exactly the same as for any shrub.

CROCKED PHILADELPHUS (Mock Orange)—Here we have a long time favorite flowering shrub which is rising to new heights of popularity with the introduction of excellent hybrids.

Mock oranges are so easy to grow that the beginner to gardening should plant two or three of them in his first group of flowering shrubs. They will grow remarkably well in a wide variety of soils and there are almost no diseases or insects that attack them.

The main thing to watch is not to let the bushes become too thick and overgrown. This can be prevented by cutting out 3 or 4 of the oldest branches as close to the ground as possible each year, once the shrubs have become well-established. The time to do this is immediately after the flowering season is finished.

The Virginal mock orange has large double pure white blooms

The Virginal mock orange

Recommended Varieties:

Snowflake — A wonderfully improved version of the fine old favorite. It is an intensely double mock orange which thrives in ordinary soil, in sun or partial shade. It makes rapid growth, and is extremely hardy. It blooms profusely in June and July and its fragrance is delightful. The dark green leaves are larger than ordinary, and cover the lower branches as well. At maturity, the bushes will be 8 feet high and approximately 6 feet across.

Virginal — One of the best and most reliable varieties available today. Lovely, large, double, pure white blooms simply cover the tall upright, yet compact plants. The main flowering season is in June and July, but this delightful variety continues to bloom at various periods throughout the remainder of the Summer and Fall. Plants

grow to about 6 feet high and 4 feet in width at maturity. It is extremely hardy, disease resistant, and grows well in just about any soil. The Virginal mock orange is ideal for the foundation bed, shrub border or for screen plantings. It also makes a fine clipped, or unclipped flowering hedge. The flowers often measure 2 inches across and are sweetly fragrant.

Golden and Green Orange Blossom Shrubs (Philadelphus Aureus and Philadelphus Coronarius) — In many parks and gardens you will often see two shrubs, one with golden colored leaves, the other with green leaves planted alternately. This presents a very striking effect, with the gold interplanted with the green. It is also an especially good arrangement for places such as in front of the veranda, or along

Coronarius, the green leaf mock orange is very fragrant

The golden leaf mock orange is fine for the foundation bed

Frosty Morn—This is a beautiful dwarf mock orange whose blossoms are pure white and very double. They have a haunting fragrance and the flowering time is late June and early July. At maturity the bushes are 3½ feet high. This is an excellent variety for landscaping around the modern ranch style homes. Hardiness is not a problem with Frosty Morn.

Belle Etoile—As you have probably already noted, most of the mock oranges are extremely fragrant, but this variety is considered to be the most highly perfumed. The star-like flowers open in lily-like fashion with the centers showing a decided light

side the house between the sidewalk and the house. Fortunately, both of these mock oranges are of the same habit and growth, and both of them grow at the same rate.

Aureus—The Aureus variety has leaves of vivid golden yellow in the Spring which gradually turn to a light green as the hot weather arrives. It makes an excellent accent color among the evergreens in the foundation planting. The creamy-white fragrant flowers appear in early June.

Coronarius—About the only difference between this and the Aureus variety is the foliage, which is a lovely blending shade of green. Creamy white flowers are produced abundantly in early June with so much fragrance that a single spray of bloom will fill a room.

Not too many people grow the buttercup bush

purple flush. The fragrance is so intense that it can be detected anywhere in the garden. Bushes are compact and orderly, and will be about 5 feet tall and 4 feet wide when fully grown.

POTENTILLA (Buttercup bush)—Not too many people are familiar with this low-growing shrub which reaches only 3 feet high, and is particularly excellent for those places in the garden where a low, brightly colored plant is needed. This is also a fine shrub for planting around the modern ranch style homes where the picture windows often come close to or reach the ground level.

Its fern-like foliage is most attractive and is borne on stems which are covered from June to October with bright golden yellow flowers that resemble buttercups.

In order to do its best, it needs a location in full sunshine, but it is not too particular about the type of soil. Have no worry about the hardiness of this delightful little shrub.

Potentilla Farreri has bright golden yellow blooms

Recommended Varieties:

Farreri — Bright golden yellow from June to October.

Katherine Dykes — Compact shrub, with arching branches, producing clear sulphur yellow flowers from July to October.

Moonlight — Pale yellow flowers from June until October.

Vilmoriana — Silvery-gray foliage and ivory tinted flowers all Summer long.

PRUNUS GLANDULOSA — (Flowering Almond) — This double flowering almond should be one of the first flowering shrubs to be planted in any garden. In the Spring even before the leaves appear, every branch of this compact little shrub is fluffy with hundreds of lovely double pink flowers which resemble miniature roses.

Flowering time is late April or early May, depending on the local climatic conditions.

Its height at maturity is 3 to 4 feet, which makes the flowering almond a very fine shrub for intermingling among the evergreens in the foundation planting, as a lawn specimen or for planting in the shrub border.

The double flowering almond is covered with fluffy pink flowers

The Rose Tree of China

being about the same size as a 50-cent piece.

Not only is this shrub a breathtaking sight in full bloom early in the Spring, but continues to be most attractive after the flowers have faded.

Its ultimate height at maturity is four to six feet. It makes an excellent lawn speci-

The purple Sand cherry has a mass of pink blooms

It prefers to be planted in a sunny location in the garden. The flowering almond should not be planted on the north side of a house, or close to a clump of trees where it will be in almost continual shade.

PRUNUS TRILOBA PLENA — (Rose Tree of China)—This member of the flowering almond family is hardier than the above-mentioned type, and will withstand really cold Winters, where the temperature consistently falls below zero. The Rose Tree of China is not only hardier, but the blooms are also larger. Beautiful double, bright pink flowers cover the long branches in April and May, each individual blossom

Spireas are extremely hardy

33

The Anthony Waterer spiraea seldom grows over 2 feet high

Bridal wreath spiraea is seen in many gardens

men and is most useful in border and bed plantings. It too needs planting in full sun.

SPIRAEA

There are many members of this widely planted family. Some have pure white flowers and others pink or red. Some have green leaves, others are yellow in color.

There are varieties that flower in the late Spring while others burst into bloom from early to late Summer.

Recommended Varieties:

Spiraea Van Houttei (Bridal Wreath) —It is generally conceded that the Bridal Wreath or Spiraea Van Houttei is one of the most popular flowering shrubs of all times. Millions of these reliable beauties have been planted all over North America. Each gracefully arching branch is covered with garlands of pure white blooms all through May and June.

It is doubtful if there is any shrub which is easier to grow or more hardy. Bridal Wreath makes an especially attractive specimen plant in the foundation bed or in the shrub border.

In the past, many people planted Bridal Wreath bushes on either side of the front steps. This proved to be a serious mistake, because as the shrub reached maturity, the arching branches spread out to almost cover the steps, ruin stockings, and drip moisture or snow, depending on the season, on any-one who entered or left the house. It is impossible to severely prune back this fine shrub, because once the lovely arching branches are cut away, its beauty will be practically destroyed.

This also happens in cases where an attempt is made to use Bridal Wreath as a clipped hedge, similar to a privet hedge. When it is kept clipped back, the graceful beauty of the branches is destroyed along with most of the flowers.

Bridal Wreath will make quite a nice looking hedge if left untrimmed, but it must be admitted that since the flowering season only lasts for two or three weeks, there is not too much point in growing it as a flowering hedge.

This excellent shrub will grow reasonably well in partial shade, although it should have full sunshine to grow and flower its best. It will grow 5 to 6 feet in height, and at maturity be almost as wide.

Be sure to prune it back one third at the time of planting. The best time to prune after that is each year following the flowering season.

Spiraea Prunifolia—A most attractive spiraea which is sometimes called double Bridal Wreath. Pure white double flowers are produced in the early Spring, soon after the golden yellow bells of forsythia appear. It puts on an excellent display, its graceful upright, slender branches being loaded with pure white, double ½ inch flowers along the upper parts of the stem. The handsome dark green foliage turns to a beautiful orange color in the Fall. Maximum height at maturity is 3 to 4 feet.

Spiraea Anthony Waterer — Here we have an ever-blooming hardy shrub which gives a good account of itself the first year after planting. It produces masses of large, showy clusters of rosy red flowers from June until frost. In order to have a succession of really top-notch flowers, the old blooms must be picked off as they fade.

Spiraea Anthony Waterer is a dependable shrub which will flower each year for many seasons. While it requires full sun to do its best, it still gives a creditable performance in partial shade.

Its low-growing habit makes it ideal for planting around the modern one story ranch style home. Foundation plantings, shrub borders and entranceways will all welcome this colorful shrub. Maximum height at maturity is 2 to 3½ feet.

This is also a shrub which must be fed regularly to maintain top size blooms. Feed it with a complete fertilizer as soon as the soil is workable in the Spring, then follow this up with another feeding about the first of July. A small handful of fertilizer should be scattered around the outside of the spiraea, and gently worked into the soil.

Spiraea Froebeli (Red spiraea)—This variety is somewhat similar to the above-mentioned Anthony Waterer spiraea, except that it grows one to two feet taller. Flowers are reddish-pink in color and produce in broad flat clusters four to five inches in diameter. Spiraea Froebeli starts to flower early in the Summer and will continue till the end of the gardening season, especially if the flower heads are removed as they fade. It will produce a beautiful display of bloom as early as the first year after planting. Do not worry about its hardiness. Although it

thrives in the sun it gives a fairly good account of itself when planted in partial shade. Again, it is an excellent flowering shrub for the foundation bed, shrub border or entrance planting.

Golden Leaf Spiraea (Physocarpus Aureus)—A most attractive spiraea which develops golden yellow foliage and large heads of whitish, and later, pinkish flowers. Flower heads are about 4 to 5 inches in diameter and start appearing in early June. The Golden Leaf spiraea makes an excellent accent plant with any of the green leaved shrubs. Maximum height is six feet and it will grow in almost any kind of soil. Hardiness is not a problem and it is extremely suitable for shrub borders and foundation plantings.

Spiraea Macrothyrsa—An everblooming pink spiraea which makes a most unusual garden shrub. Imagine a six foot plant laden with cameo pink blossoms, borne in spikes which often measure 12 inches in length. These are carried on strong, upright four foot stems. If the blooms are removed as they fade, others just as large will take their place all Summer long. It is an excellent grower, with good foliage and is attacked by few, if any, insect pests. Requires an ordinary soil, and will stand some shade.

Winter honeysuckle

35

Golden flame honeysuckle can be trained to climb a wall

handsome, upright shrubs are covered with clusters of rose-red flowers in June and July, growing to a maximum height of 5 to 7 feet at maturity. The foliage is an attractive bluish-green in color. The extremely fragrant flowers are followed by bright red berries which supply an abundance of food for the birds. This red-flowering honeysuckle is very hardy and will survive the Winters where the temperature dips below the zero mark quite often.

It is wonderful for screens, hedges or backgrounds where a tall, fast-growing shrub is needed. It is not the slightest bit particular about the type of soil and does well even in semi-shade conditions. When grown as a hedge, it is best to start with small sized plants, setting them one foot apart.

LONICERA FRAGRANTISSIMA (Winter honeysuckle)—This is the shrub which brings the first breath of Spring to the garden each year. In the south, it is almost evergreen, while in the north, the creamy white fragrant flowers start to appear in March and April, depending on the season

Caryopteris (Blue Mist spiraea) — It is a wonderful addition to the color parade of low-growing shrubs. It will be literally covered with lovely powdery blue fringed flowers from August until heavy frost. The dwarf growing plants are perfectly round, measuring two feet in diameter and growing 1½ to 2 feet tall. Foliage is colored a cool silvery green, and the plants are quite bushy.

Blue Mist requires about the same Winter protection as buddleia. Make a good sized mound of soil around the base of the bushes just before freeze-up time. This fine shrub prefers a sandy loam soil, and requires full sun to grow and flower well. It will produce considerably more bloom if cut back severely each Spring. This shrub is recommended for Spring planting only.

LONICERA ZABELLI (Red Flowering honeysuckle)—It is hard to beat this new red honeysuckle for bloom and perfume. It is wonderful for both color and fragrance where a taller shrub is required. These

Sweet honeysuckle produces pink trumpet-shaped flowers

36

and the local climate. It grows six to eight feet high and is very useful in tall foundation plantings, shrub borders, hedges and screen plantings.

The shiny foliage makes an excellent addition to cool-looking bouquets and flower arrangements during the Summer months. You will find it a fast and vigorous grower.

LONICERA CLAVEY'S DWARF —
Many fast growing shrubs have more faults than good points, but Clavey's Dwarf honeysuckle is the exception to this rule. It will make a lovely dwarf hedge the first year you plant it and then will grow thicker in the years to follow. Grows about 3 feet high and 3 feet wide but has to be trimmed. Small creamy white flowers appear in the Spring, followed by masses of red berries. Foliage is thick and colored a deep lush green. Hardiness is not a problem and it grows in almost any type of soil, but needs a sunny location.

LONICERA GOLD FLAME HONEY-
SUCKLE—From June until freeze-up, this magnificent vine is covered with showy clusters of large, fragrant flowers which are colored rosy red on the outside and gold on the inside. They are trumpet shaped, and the attractive, rich blue-green foliage makes an effective background for these brilliant flowers. Thrives in full sun or partial shade, and can be used in many places around the garden—trellises, porches, pergolas, fences or for covering a bank. It also can be trained to grow as a shrub.

LONICERA TATARICA — (Sweet
Honeysuckle) — Bushes are covered with dainty, small pink trumpet-shaped flowers in May, followed by an abundance of bright red berries. The sweet honeysuckle makes a large shrub and will eventually grow to 6 to 8 feet in both height and width. It will thrive in the poorest soil, and is excellent for screening and specimen planting.

TAMARIX (Tamarisk) — An exciting
Summer flowering shrub which is covered with lovely rose-pink flower clusters in June and early July. Not only are the flowers lacy and spike-shaped, but the silvery blue-green foliage makes a tremendous feathery background for them. Both the flowers and stems are excellent for cutting. Plants have great hardiness and are

Viburnums are decorative and useful in the home garden

The Japanese snowball has perfectly round pure white flowers

about six feet high when fully grown. Fine for large foundation plantings, shrub borders and screening. It is also beautiful as a lawn specimen.

This shrub is also excellent for lakeshore or seashore gardens, being very tolerant to salt air and wind.

The tamarix must be cut back to six or eight inches when transplanted, or it may not grow.

VIBURNUM (Snowball) — The viburnum or snowball family comprises a large group of shrubs which are among the most decorative and useful plants for the home garden. Most of them have an extremely compact and bushy growth, lovely flowers, and in many instances the foliage produces some of the most brilliant color in the Fall. Most members of this family are not the slightest bit particular about the type of soil in which they are planted, except that it should contain enough humus

or organic matter to keep it moist. In situations where the soil tends to be on the dry side, it is advisable to add extra humus before planting and then to cover the soil surrounding each viburnum with a mulch at least 2 to 3 inches deep.

Recommended Varieties:

Viburnum Carlcephalum (Fragrant viburnum) — There is little doubt that this fragrant viburnum is one of the finest of all the flowering shrubs. If you are a lover of perfume in the garden — and who isn't — then you will want to include this most sweet-smelling of all shrubs in your garden. It comes to our gardens from England where it originated just before World War II. It is absolutely hardy, and has gone through several Winters with the temperatures measuring 10 to 20° below zero.

Flowers measure 4 to 6 inches across, and the color is a lovely white, tinged with reddish pink. The clusters of bloom com-

pletely cover the bushes. Ultimately, the plants will grow 6 feet in height. The handsome, deep green foliage is brilliantly colored in the Fall. Flowering time is late May and early June. This shrub is not bothered seriously by any insects, and is very easy to transplant and grow.

Viburnum Burkwoodi — Here is a very easy-to-grow shrub which will thrive in places lacking in sunlight and in smoky cities and towns. Flowers are waxy, blush white and delicately perfumed. They appear in the early Spring, just as the leaves are starting to unfold. Their gardenia-like fragrance is so sweet that it will fill the average small garden.

Bushes grow about 6 feet high, and 4 to 5 feet in diameter. They like a well-drained location, but the soil should contain plenty of moisture. Foliage remains a shiny dark green all Summer long, and then turns to brilliant colors in the Fall.

Viburnum Carlesi — For many years, this has been one of the most popular of the early Spring flowering shrubs. It bursts into bloom with the tulips, and spreads its haunting fragrance throughout the garden. The beautiful waxy-white blooms are at their best just as the leaves start to open. Carlesi will grow 5 to 6 feet high at maturity.

Viburnum Tomentosum Plicatum (Japanese Snowball) — This new strain of Japanese snowball is a lovely sight. The bushes are stately, erect growers, dressed in beautiful green foliage. Its pure white flowers are arranged in a perfectly round ball, 3 to 4 inches across. There are few June flowering shrubs to match the rare beauty of this lovely plant. The tight flower heads are a cream color at first but later turn to a lovely white and are borne in opposite pairs the entire length of the branches.

In the Fall the leaves turn deep red before dropping from the bushes. At maturity the bushes will be six to eight feet in height depending on the soil and climatic conditions.

Viburnum Opulus Sterile (White Snowball)—A favorite flowering shrub for many years. Blooms resembling showy snowballs cover the tall-growing plant from late June until the middle of July. The white

The red berries of the High Bush cranberry last all winter

when its beautiful blossom is replaced by immense clusters of half-inch golden yellow fruits. A tremendous number of heavy clusters are produced, creating a beautiful show against the rich green foliage. The heavily fruited branches are excellent for indoor decoration and combine handsomely with gladiolus, dahlias or chrysanthemums.

Bushes are easily grown and are as hardy as any oak tree.

Viburnum Opulus (High Bush Cranberry) — The high bush cranberry is one of the hardiest and finest shrubs for adding beauty and charm to the garden, the year round, and is one of the best shrubs for attracting the birds. This upright spreading shrub covered with deep green 3-lobed leaves, makes the perfect background and is admirably suited for screening. The flowers are white and showy, but it is the spectacular red berries which are of particular interest to the gardener. The heavy clusters of scarlet red berries remain on the bushes into the Winter, and are a truly spectacular sight when seen against a back-

snowball is a dependable shrub which through the years has been proven hardy in all climatic zones. It is disease resistant, easy to grow and transplants well. Eventually grows six to eight feet in height. Again, the leaves turn a brilliant deep red color in the Fall.

Viburnum Opulus Nanum (Hedge Viburnum)—Here we have a dwarf, stubby plant which never grows over two feet high. It is particularly well adapted for edgings and hedges in wet or heavy clay ground where it is difficult for other plants to thrive. It grows well in light shade, and is extremely hardy. It can be clipped or left to grow naturally, as desired. In either case, it grows into a fine compact and low hedge which requires little care.

Viburnum Opulus Xanthocarpum (Golden Cranberry Bush)—This makes a handsome bush 5 to 7 feet high. It is particularly attractive from July to December

Viburnum Dantatum

The showy white flowers of the Viburnum Opulus are followed by spectacular red berries

WEIGELA

The weigelas are a group of useful and most attractive flowering shrubs which can be in flower in May, in June or in July. Their flowers have somewhat the same shape as a foxglove, and appear in profusion. They like the soil to be moist, and to contain a large amount of humus. They resent the shade, or roots of large trees. Most varieties grow from 5 to 6 feet in height when fully grown.

Recommended Varieties:

Weigela Bristol Ruby — One of the showiest and most brilliant of all the flowering shrubs. Ruby red bell-like blooms are produced in huge clusters during June and continue to show on the plant at various periods during the mid-summer and Autumn seasons. The best way of insuring late

ground of white snow. They are slightly bitter and are usually ignored by the birds in the Fall, but are eaten during the Winter and so provide a very useful and emergency supply of food. Woodpeckers, ruffled grouse and many other birds welcome the fruit when the snow is on the ground and little other food is available.

The foliage grows right to the ground, and this makes the high bush cranberry a much better-than-average hedge plant. It responds well to trimming, or can be left to grow as a natural hedge, varying from 3 to 10 feet in height. There is hardly any other shrub which is hardier than this versatile member of the viburnum family.

Viburnum Mariesi — This flowering shrub has been hailed by many people to be lovelier than the dogwood. It is a truly magnificent shrub of medium size which should be grown in every garden. The outer "lace cap", with large pure white blossoms surrounds the small fertile ones which fill the center. Later in the season the blossoms are replaced by brilliant red berries, which are accented by the lovely green foliage. Viburnum Mariesi grows six to seven feet high.

Weigelas do best in moist soil

40

season bloom is to give them a feeding with a complete fertilizer in the early Spring. The plants of Bristol Ruby have a well rounded shape, and grow to about 5 feet in height. The foliage is a lovely dark green, and the bushes require very little pruning as they flower equally well from the old or new wood. It is especially attractive as a lawn specimen, or set among other shrubs in the foundation bed or shrub border. If left untrimmed, it will also make a lovely tall hedge.

Avalanche—This is the best pure white weigela. In late Spring and early Summer it is a beautiful sight to behold with its thousands of pure white, trumpet-like blooms. Avalanche makes a fine contrast when planted alongside Bristol Ruby.

Weigela Eva Rathke — Here we have another fine hybrid weigela which produces thousands of bright vibrant red trumpet shaped flowers. It blooms in the late Spring, and more or less continuously throughout the Summer. Height at maturity will vary from 3 to 5 feet. It will thrive in a variety of soils, requires little care, and is content in any climate.

Weigela Pink (Rosea) — From far away Asia comes this graceful shrub with long arching branches. No other shrub surpasses the pink weigela in the beauty and profusion of its trumpet-shaped blossoms. Flowering time is late May or early June, when long sprays of pink flowers form against a background of lovely dark green foliage.

Bristol Ruby weigela is a brilliant red shrub

Dwarf shrubs

The modern ranch style home has created a demand for dwarf shrubs and evergreens which will not block windows or hide its features. In many cases we no longer have a high foundation wall which must be screened by tall growing shrubs and evergreens to prevent an otherwise garden eyesore.

With this type of house there is no point in planting tall growing evergreens or shrubs, thinking they can be kept low by heavy and repressive pruning. The results of this treatment will only be a group of heavy and unattractive stumps at the ground level.

Certainly the ranch style house and others built low to the ground do not need as much planting as houses that stand high out of the ground, but they do require some planting. Without it they appear stark and alone on their site.

Best evergreen for planting in these circumstances is the dwarf Japanese yew (Taxus Cuspidata Nana). There is also a tall growing form so make sure you obtain the dwarf or Nana variety. It can be kept in bounds almost as easily as a privet hedge and takes well to clipping. This evergreen will grow well and retain its dark green color in both sun and shade.

A very effective contrast with the dark green of the yews can be made by planting the red-leaved Japanese barberry alongside. It also takes well to clipping, but in order to preserve as much as possible of the natural flowing lines of this attractive shrub, do only enough clipping to keep it within reasonable bounds. Depending on the growing soil conditions, the Japanese barberry will grow from three to five feet high.

There is an intriguing dwarf form of red barberry which has just been introduced recently from Holland. Its name is Crimson Pygmy. It grows five to eight inches high and 15 to 24 inches across. Be sure and grow it in full sun if you want this new shrub to show its reddest color.

Another low-growing shrub that is a favorite is the firethorn or pyracantha. It grows four to six feet high and flowers in May. The attractive long trusses of pure white flowers are only a prelude to the big show. An abundance of brilliant orange-scarlet berries follow the bloom. The bush becomes a mound of flame with the effect lasting well into the Winter.

The cotoneasters is of great value when planted in foundation beds around ranch style homes. There are several ground hugging (prostrate) forms, and they are also useful in the rock garden or as a ground cover on the side of a hill.

One of the most widely planted of the cotoneasters is the variety Horizontalis. Leaves are a shining green, growing about a half an inch long. They turn a brilliant

Cotoneasters are valuable in the foundation bed

fire red in the Fall before they finally drop off the spreading branches. At the same time the branches are also covered with bright red fruit. Pretty pinkish white flowers cover the branches in late Spring.

Hedges

Planting a hedge is one of the first jobs to be done in landscaping a property, and like many other aspects of a hedge should be properly planned. Aside from the trees, hedges are one of the most permanent parts of the garden. Poor planning and planting in the beginning can spell trouble year after year.

Any hedge should improve the attractiveness of the grounds surrounding the home.

Well-kept, healthy hedges are things of beauty in themselves, especially when they are combined correctly with other landscape plantings. Hedges are used as living fences to mark boundaries between properties, divisions between the front and the backyard, to suitably enclose backyards, and as background plantings for low-growing shrubs and flower beds.

Tall hedges, either trimmed or untrimmed are used as screens to cut off unsightly buildings or views.

Stress Short Roots

What type of hedge plant should I choose? In making this important decision be sure and select types that have short fibrous roots which do not extend more than two or three feet beyond the hedge plants.

Such hedges will not rob the surrounding garden of plant food and moisture to any great extent.

Many home gardeners, since the end of World War II have had the sad experience of planting a fast-growing hedge of Chinese elm. It is really a fast-growing *tree* which will eventually grow 60 feet in height if treated as a tree. After six or seven years the trunk starts to broaden out and fails to throw out branches near the ground level which means that you no longer have a nice solid green wall. At the same time ,the roots will be reaching out as much as 25 to 50 feet on either side of the hedge to rob the surrounding garden of much of nutriment and moisture.

Of course if you have to look upon an unsightly scene close by your garden then you will want to hide it quickly and there is no doubt that the Chinese elm will do a job under such circumstances. However, it is preferable to use the common Persian lilac or the high bush cranberry if you want to hide something quickly. These have the typical short, fibrous roots of the shrub, and will not rob the surrounding area of moisture and plant food.

Rose multiflora makes a good farm hedge, but is definitely not recommended for the average-sized garden in the city and suburbs.

In the past couple of years there have been some ever-blooming roses introduced such as County Fair, which make excellent flowering hedges, or fence roses. County Fair's dainty pink buds and self-cleaning flowers are constantly in mass bloom from early Spring until Fall.

Planting

The preparation of the soil and planting procedure for a hedge would be the same as for any shrub.

Set the plants 6 to 18 inches apart, depending on the size and variety of plant you choose.

A newly planted hedge will usually be about 12 to 15 inches high, depending on the variety. At this stage you must be ruthless and cut down the plants to within six inches of the ground. The beginner may be reluctant to cut his new hedge so severely, but the later results will prove such action to be well worthwhile. Prune two or three more times during the first season, but not after the middle of August. The pruning forces the bushes to thicken out considerably near the base, and help form a good framework for the years to come.

Pruning

Hedges should always be pruned so that they are wider at the bottom than at the top. It is unfortunate that the natural tendency of any hedge plant is to grow just the opposite. If you allow hedge plants to grow wider at the top than the bottom, the sunshine and moisture will not be able to reach the bottom of the hedge.

Once the hedge gets out of hand, a series of gaps will develop, because the bottom of the hedge will fail to throw out branches, and so your hedge will no longer be symmetrical from top to bottom. In pruning the hedge, it is also a good plan to taper or round off the top to prevent the snow from collecting on its top. A heavy snow storm can often break down a hedge which is flat on top and this type of damage will spoil the appearance for two or three years.

The first Spring after planting, cut the hedge to a height of one foot before the leaves appear. In June begin regularly trimming and shaping as you did the first year. After three or four years, you should

The most all purpose hedge is Amur River privet

have a hedge three feet in height, two feet wide at the bottom, and 18 inches wide at the top.

Starting with the first year after planting, established hedges should be given a feeding with a complete fertilizer just as soon as the soil can be worked in the Spring. Apply the fertilizer at the rate of 4 pounds per 100 square feet of hedge row. Scatter it on both sides of the hedge and gently work it into the soil.

In hot, dry weather, it is a good plan to lay one of the plastic or canvas soaker hoses along the bottom of the hedge and let the water gently ooze into the soil.

AMUR RIVER PRIVET — The most useful all-purpose hedge for most gardens is the Amur River privet. It grows fairly quickly and has the desired short fibrous roots. The bushes can easily be kept in shape and maintained at any height, short or tall. If left unpruned, it will grow to 10 feet in height. Regular pruning or shearing twice each Summer will produce a perfectly even surface. A single row of plants will make a good hedge, but an even fuller and more compact one can be made by planting

The Japanese barberry makes a colorful hedge

The Alpine currant is an excellent low growing hedge for shady locations

green barberry turns red in the Fall, while the red variety has a brilliant red color all Summer long.

ALPINE CURRANT is excellent for a low-growing hedge in a shady location, and it will grow well in cities where there is considerable smoke and car fumes.

This fine plant has a dwarf compact habit and keeps a very symmetrical appearance. In May or early June the bushes are covered with fragrant yellow flowers.

LAUREL LEAF WILLOW — If you want a tall screen, say 10 to 14 feet high, and one that will grow quickly in a wet spot, or in poor soil, then the Laurel Leaf willow is the shrub for you to buy. The leaves are very attractive, and so glossy that they appear to be varnished. You will find their dark green color most attractive. The Laurel Leaf willow is very hardy and easy to grow. Left unclipped, it is vase-shaped. Plant 3 to 5 feet apart when using it for screening purposes.

IBOLIUM PRIVET — A choice new hybrid variety that is very popular — lush deep green foliage. Plants grow so well that a row planted as wide as 12 inches apart will still produce a thick hedge. Privet gives that extra look of distinction, outlines the boundaries of your property, preserving your own privacy. It is a fast-growing variety and with it you can have a hedge quickly. Requires just enough trimming to maintain the shape you want—once or twice yearly is usually sufficient.

two rows zig-zag, at the apex of a 9 inch triangle. In the Winter the black berries of the Amur River privet are most attractive to the birds. The glossy green foliage usually stays on the bushes until after Christmas.

JAPANESE BARBERRY (Green or red) — For a low-growing hedge along driveways, or to keep people and animals off your lawn, the red or green Japanese barberry is excellent. Either color of barberry will be one of the most useful, easiest to grow, and abuse-absorbing hedges that money can buy.

Barberry will grow in almost any location or type of soil. Maximum height is 3 feet but can be kept lower by heavy pruning. Set the plants nine inches apart, either in a single row, or in the zig-zag fashion recommended for the Amur River privet. The

Barberry has green or red leaves

Ibolium privet has lush green foliage

TREES

TREES

A well placed shade tree can be a source of year-round enjoyment

There is no greater natural asset to property than trees, they add beauty, form windbreaks, give shade, privacy and an extensive variety of color, and incidentally add value to your home.

Trees serve to blend the house and the surrounding landscape together as if they had existed for many years. They also provide an effective background to the home. The various shapes of the individual trees create a great deal of the attractiveness and the beauty found in a garden. Trees provide shade on the hot Summer days, and colour the year round. It would be impossible to imagine a garden without at least three or four shade, flowering or fruit trees.

In selecting suitable locations for various trees, the best plan is to keep the taller ones to the sides and rear of the property. It's a good plan to look out through the windows when selecting choice locations for trees. By doing this, you will be able to choose planting sites that will not only provide garden beauty, but also frame or add to the view as seen from indoors.

Plan before you plant—A well placed shade tree in a garden can be a source of year around enjoyment, not only for the home owner and family, but for those who visit or just pass by. On the other hand, trees planted in the wrong spots end up as nothing but a nuisance.

Before planting study carefully the pros and cons of the tree in which you are interested. What are the rooting and branching habits, how tall will it be at maturity, is it able to stand up to the weather, smog, insects and diseases? Your final choice must be a tree you can manage within your parcular circumstances. It is obvious the gardener with an average sized lot will be restricted to trees fairly small in size, easily pruned and otherwise maintained.

Beware of the pitfalls. A great favourite, the weeping willow, eventually develops a root system larger than the average house, so don't plant one on the corner of your house or adjacent to a drainage system!

It may be repetitious, but please watch those hydro and telephone wires, your house and neighbours' property when planting taller trees, it can be very disappointing to have branches lopped off or even the whole tree removed.

A blue spruce, or a fast growing pine, planted in front of windows will soon force you to remove it. "Think before you plant", is a good resolution for the trees.

Air conditioning with shade trees — The hot Summer sun can be very uncomfortable without adequate shade on your property. The answer is in placing shade trees in a position that gives utmost protection from the sun. Plant the trees at some distance from the place to be shaded, slightly north of due west. If you plant the tree, or trees, right over the spot, the shade will fall to the east of it in the afternoon.

The hottest part of the Summer day is usually in the mid and late afternoon, when the sun's rays slant considerably. To combat this, plant far enough to the west so the tree will intercept the slanted rays and the shade fall on the desired area.

For shade directly over outdoor living areas at mid-day, the tree should be planted at the edge of the area, but not where an outdoor fireplace will scorch leaves on the lower branches.

The same rules hold true for shade on a terrace or patio. If the terrace is on the east side of the house only the directly overhead sun needs to be screened off because the house will shade the terrace in the afternoon. In this case the shade tree can be right beside the patio or terrace to guard against the mid-day sun. But if the patio is on the west side of the house, two trees may be needed, one at some distance to the west to block the hot afternoon sun and one close to the patio to intercept the sun's rays at mid-day and up to the middle of the afternoon.

Shade trees can make a difference of 4 to 10 degrees in the temperature of the outdoor living area. This can mean the difference on a hot Summer day between comfort and discomfort. Correctly located shade

Trees blend the house and surrounding landscape together as if they had existed for many years

trees will also eliminate the harsh glare of the sun.

These suggestions for locating shade trees can also be used to make various rooms inside the house more comfortable by shading the wall of the house and one or more windows from the hot afternoon sun.

How to plant a shade tree — Every Spring the nurseryman gets a lot of blame he doesn't deserve when a shade or flowering tree fails to grow. Most failures along this line are due to poor planting methods by the home gardener.

Is it worth taking the time to plant a tree correctly? The answer is a loud and resounding "yes".

Your trees are an important physical and financial asset. It's a proven fact that homes surrounded by good trees sell faster and at 15 to 20 percent higher prices.

Proper planting of a tree doesn't mean just digging a hole, placing the tree in it and filling up that hole with soil. If possible, it will pay you to go out to the nursery or garden center and pick your own tree, bring it directly home and plant it. While at the garden center you can obtain the ingredients you don't have at home which are necessary to get the tree off to a good start. These include a good soil mixture to replace the soil removed when digging the planting hole, some peat moss, a bag of complete plant food or fertilizer, and a wooden stake to hold the tree upright.

Before you leave the nursery or garden center make sure that the roots are completely covered with damp burlap so they won't dry out in the sun and wind on the way home. More trees fail to grow because the

Good drainage is necessary for shade trees

roots are allowed to dry out before planting than any other cause. Trees are always shipped balled and burlapped. Do not remove the burlap but plant as soon as possible after you bring the tree home from the nursery, or it is delivered to your house. This could mean ordering the planting materials mentioned before, several days ahead of the expected arrival of the tree.

If you *cannot* plant right away then heel the tree out in the garden until you can. Heeling-in simply means the storing of a dormant plant, like a tree, in a trench until conditions are favourable for planting. Just dig a trench twelve to fifteen inches deep making one side vertical and one side a long slope. Across the slope lay the tree with the roots extending to the bottom of the trench and facing the vertical side. Before heeling-in newly received trees and shrubs be sure to remove all packing material. Fill in the whole trench, gradually adding soil and firming it around the roots to prevent air spaces.

Nursery stock can be left in such a trench for as long as two or three weeks without harm but the sooner you can plant the better.

When it comes to the actual planting, make sure you dig a hole large enough to accommodate the roots without cramping them. The soil you remove should be discarded and replaced with a soil mixture consisting of three parts good garden loam, two parts peat moss and one part coarse sand. In the bottom of the hole, place two handfuls of a complete plant food or fertilizer and cover this with two inches of the soil mixture. Then make a mound of soil in the bottom of the hole to bring the soil level up to planting depth. The tree should be planted about an inch deeper than the planting depth at the nursery. This is the time also to put the stake for the tree in place. By doing this now you will avoid damaging the roots later on.

Next add three or four inches of the soil mixture and thoroughly tramp or firm this around the roots so there will be no air spaces. Experience shows you can do this best by stamping with your feet right in the hole. But don't try to firm the soil into brick. Add another two or three inches of soil and firm again. Then fill the hole with water and let this drain completely away before adding the remainder of the soil.

The tree is going to require plenty of water so leave a saucer-shaped depression around the trunk of the tree for watering purposes. It won't hurt to water the tree every day for the first two or three months but whatever you do, don't let the roots dry out.

A piece of an old rubber tire tube makes an excellent way of tying the tree to the stake. In making this tie, be sure that you don't have it so tight that it will girdle the tree as it grows.

Good drainage is essential — Many shade trees fail to grow well in the home garden because of poor drainage. For this reason, homeowners frequently have difficulty in establishing trees in areas where the soil consists largely of heavy clay subsoil turned up in the building of their houses.

Lightening heavy clay soil around a tree's root zone by the addition of peat moss, material from the home compost heap, or other forms of humus at planting time may not help the drainage problem. In some cases it can make matters worse. If the water cannot penetrate the surrounding clay, it may gather around the tree's roots and be trapped there. This is like planting a tree in a bucket of water, and few trees will survive such treatment.

A good way to test for bad drainage is to dig a hole about 18 inches deep in the spot where you are planning to plant a tree. Fill the hole with water and allow it to stand for 36 hours. If water remains in the hole at the end of that time without replenishment from rain or other sources, then the drainage is unsatisfactory.

Here are several things to remedy this situation. Perhaps the surface of the ground can be regraded to encourage better runoff. Or, if there is a lower surface level nearby, drain tiles can be laid to carry water from the bottom of the planting hole to a lower spot where it will run away. This, of course requires digging a trench to lay the drain tile—a difficult job if the distance is great. Another method, which may be better in some instances, is to dig the planting hole somewhat deeper than necessary to accommodate the roots and fill the bottom with a generous layer of coarse gravel. This will allow room for water to stand where it will not touch the tree roots. If surface runoff is slow, soil should be mounded around the base of the tree to keep water from gathering there. And sometimes it is better to fill the hole with the same dirt that was taken out so as not to encourage standing water in the tree's root zone.

Feeding shade and fruit trees — Very few home gardeners ever bother to feed their trees, they just plant them and expect them to grow well for the rest of their life. This is a fallacy because there is not an inexhaustible supply of plant food in the soil. Each year as the roots of the trees take up the food in soluble form, the amount of plant food is diminished, never to be replaced unless you do it.

What will happen if you give a mature tree a feeding? If it hasn't been fed for some time it will usually grow two to three feet the first year after feeding! One of the very best ways of keeping insect pests and diseases to a minimum is to feed your shade and fruit trees regularly.

Feeding time is either in the month of April or during October.

"For small trees" the best method is to broadcast a complete fertilizer in a circle on the ground beneath the outer spread of the branches.

"To feed bigger trees" you need to drill a series of holes beneath the outer spread of branches. Make the holes 2 inches in diameter, 18 inches deep and 18 inches apart. Feeding a larger tree this way is quite a job but there are no halfway measures. All too often, home gardeners try to get by with a few holes in the sod which means that very few of the feeding roots get correct nourishment.

Most trees have a root system at least as wide as their branch spread, with the majority of the feeding roots within a circle on or just beyond the drip line. What's a drip line? It's the circle described by the arching branches of the trees. Drill the holes in

This is what happens when the taller trees are not kept to the sides and rear of the property

Before planting find out the rooting and branching habits of a tree

staggered fashion. Take some sand or dry soil and mix it half and half with the complete fertilizer and fill up the holes.

Fruit trees also need an annual feeding. This is usually done by the broadcast method. In other words you scatter the fertilizer in a wide band around the trees at the drip line. Make a start about half way between the trunk and the end of the limbs and extend about the same distance beyond the ends of the limbs.

Fertilizing trees in the lawn — If the fruit or other trees are planted as lawn specimens, make sure the grass is dry before applying the fertilizer or some burning of the grass can take place. It's also a wise plan to sweep the lawn with a broom or the back of a rake to knock any lumps of fertilizer off the grass. Get out the hose and thoroughly soak the fertilizer into the ground.

Fruit trees — Mature apple trees 15 years or older should be fed 10 to 12 lbs of fertilizer per tree. 6 to 8 lbs is required

by the average 10 year old peach tree. Plums, pears and cherries will require less, say 5 to 6 lbs per tree.

Raising the soil level around trees— How high can soil be raised around a tree without injuring it? The answer to this lies in the type of the soil surrounding the tree. Where the soil is light and well drained, the level of the soil around the tree can be raised as much as a foot with very little injury or harm. On the other hand, in heavy clay and not well drained soil, raising the grade as little as six inches can cause injury. This really has the effect of strangling the tree.

If you wish to get a satisfactory slope for the lawn, and this means raising the existing level of soil around a tree or trees, your only answer is to build a loose stone or brick wall around the trunk which will allow air and moisture to reach the roots. Such a wall is often called a "well", and its diameter should be four times the diameter of the trunk. For instance, if the tree trunk is 2 feet in diameter, then that of the well should be 8 feet. Any well that needs to be more

On a hot summer day shade can mean the difference between comfort and discomfort

prevent infection by disease and to stop insect pests from gaining an easy entry into the tree. In giving the tree the right treatment it may be necessary to be quite ruthless. Jagged breaks or abrasions should first of all be cut clean with a sharp knife or saw. It's important to clear away all dead or diseased portions of the wood or bark. Often this requires cutting off branches or limbs, or cutting out diseased portions.

As a general rule (except for the most minor cuts or breaks) it pays to call in a reliable and recognized tree expert.

Wounds should be sterilized, especially older ones which have become infected.

Getting rid of tree stumps — Tree stumps have the habit of turning up in the strangest places. They always seem to be present in the middle of the garden, lawn or in the middle of a field where we have to go around them. Getting rid of such a stump usually takes a lot of work and it can be seldom done quickly.

One of the easiest solutions, if the stump is in the middle of the garden or along the side, is to dress it up by placing a flower box or container on top. Such a box or container would have to be at least 8 inches deep and will need filling with a good soil mixture to within 1 inch of the top. The space at the top is left to permit adequate watering. You can either make up your own soil mixture consisting of three parts good top soil, one part humus, and one part sand, or you can buy one of the commercially prepared soils at your nearby nursery or garden center. When you prepare your own soil mixture, be sure and add a tablespoonful of complete fertilizer for each quart of soil used.

The box could be painted white or a colour that would match the colour scheme of your house or garage. Painting the stump is not advised, as it looks much better if it's left in its natural state. A good looking combination of flowers for such a flower box could consist of three or four either pink or red geraniums, two or three White Satin petunias, and some trailing blue lobelia. There are two kinds of lobelia usually sold, so be sure and ask for the trailing kind. They will trail down over the sides of the box and in combination with the generaniums and petunias make a most attractive picture.

than 2 feet deep will need tile drains running out horizontally from the bottom. Be sure you don't narrow the well at the top when building it or you will have difficulty each year cleaning out leaves and other debris.

Metal tree guards — The only sure way of protecting shade, fruit and flowering trees when they're small is to use metal tree guards. These will not only serve to protect the trees from rabbit or mice injuries, but will give good protection from mower damage during the Summer months.

These metal tree guards should be extended into the ground for at least 2 inches. This will help to deter rodents from burrowing down under the wire guard. Unfor-

tunately, some of them get over-ambitious and do get underneath the guard. You can prevent this by placing crushed stones, cinders or coarse gravel around the base of the tree. Make this layer 1½ to 2 inches deep.

Be sure and practise clean cultivation by keeping grass or straw mulch away from these tree guards. This will go a long way in discouraging the mice from burrowing into the mulch and finally getting at the bark of the tree and girdling it.

Tree wounds and their treatment — Most persons don't realize it's just as easy to injure a tree trunk or a branch as it is a human being. Any wounds or cuts on a tree need the same prompt treatment to

50

Homes surrounded by trees sell faster at 15% to 20% higher prices.

it means a terrible waste of one of nature's most abundant fertilizers. The best plan of course is to place the leaves that fall on your property into your own compost heap. If that is not possible please don't burn them but see the leaves are made available either to the city or to a neighbour who could use them.

"Every garden should have its own compost heap." In it is broken down into humus a host of waste materials including grass cuttings, leaves (except oak), vegetables, vines, flower stalks and weeds. From the house come citrus fruit peel, discarded vegetable leaves such as lettuce, cabbage and cauliflower, potato peelings, carrots, turnips, parsnips, beets etc. In addition, you can also add faded flowers and hulls from strawberries; in fact, any leafy vegetable and flower refuse.

You may ask, "Why go to all this trouble? Just pop it into the garbage and forget about it." But this is breaking one of the fundamental laws of conservation. In the production of flowers, leaves, trunks and branches, fruits and vegetables, plant food and other material is taken from the soil and also the soil's vital supply of humus is used up. Unless this is replaced the soil becomes gradually poorer and eventually almost useless. That's the story of the agriculture of many past civilizations. When the soil goes, so does the power and influence of

Removing tree stumps with a chemical—A garden problem which creates a great deal of difficulty for many city and town gardeners is the removal of a tree stump where it is impossible to use a bulldozer or any heavy machinery. Spring is the time to do something about it.

The first step is to bore a vertical hole, one and a half inches in diameter and eighteen inches deep in the center of the stump. In it pour one and a half ounces of salt peter, which is uusally available at the corner drug store. Fill the remainder of the hole with water and plug tightly. Next Spring remove the plug and pour ten ounces of coal oil into the hole and ignite. You will find the stump will smoulder away even to the ends of the roots without blazing, and nothing but ashes will be left.

What to do with leaves—The smell of burning leaves seems to be a wonderful perfume to some people. But to many more

Immediate beauty and shade can be secured by moving into place a large size tree

a nation and its standard of living.

The best way of keeping up a good supply of humus in the soil is to add to it each year valuable humus manufactured in the home compost heap.

Perhaps the easiest way of making one is to use cement blocks. A good average size for most gardens would be six feet long and four feet wide. The blocks can be bought and added to the compost box as it is filled. Down through the middle of the four corner blocks drive iron pipes or stakes to hold the box reasonably rigid.

Some people have used scrap lumber and even snow fences to good advantage, others swear by plaster lathes. The kind of siding you use to enclose the material really doesn't matter so long as it keeps the heap neat and tidy.

In using the cement blocks put the first rectangular layer in place. Leave one end open at the start so you can dump the material in easily. As you add the material, tramp it down until you have a layer six inches deep. Soak it with water. Now do the whole process again until you have another six inch layer. Again soak with water. Additional cement blocks may be added as needed.

The composting of leaves and other leafy material from the garden can be hurried up by turning the material every two days and seeing that the moisture content remains high. This can be an advantage early in the gardening season, because the humus so created can be used in a number of ways around the garden. However, in the case of leaves in the Fall, the gardening season is just about at an end, making speed unnecessary. The leaves can be added to the compost heap as outlined above, and by the time Spring arrives, they will have decomposed into the desired form of humus.

Think before you cut down any tree —During the outward growth of cities and towns, ground is greedily gobbled up for housing and ever growing industry. Among the victims of this expansion are our trees.

It isn't often nowadays that we can drive around newly forming suburbs and see that the trees have been spared. Most have been ruthlessly swept away. Yet their inspiring majesty, form and dignity takes years to formulate. The beauty of our wooded developments is so obvious when compared to those whose lots have been denuded.

What chance has a one hundred year old tree against a bulldozer? When we consider that trees are a part of our heritage and must be cherished, the question arises as to the awareness of our real estate sub-dividers to their responsibilities not only to the present, but to the future.

In all fairness the home buyer should be prepared to pay just a little more for his house in order to preserve the trees standing on the lot. The extra cost is so very low in comparison to the money needed to replant the property with suitable trees that it is hard to imagine anyone quibbling.

Subdividers would be well advised to retain the services of a reliable firm of tree experts before they commit a new building area to the onslaught of the bulldozer.

Many other subdivisions have been built through necessity on farm land denuded of trees by previous generations. Here we have the opportunity to do ourselves and the future generations a real service by replanting the trees. We say future generations because in many cases the trees we plant will not reach anywhere near maturity in our lifetime.

Immediate shade can be secured by moving into place a large-sized tree. What is the best size for this purpose? Tree experts regard one with a trunk from 4 to 6 inches in diameter and 18 to 20 feet in height as the ideal size for this purpose. Moving such trees will cost money, but not as much as you might think. Especially when you consider the extra value it will add to the property. No other kind of landscaping will add so much value for money spent. Costs will vary depending where you live, but make sure you are doing business with the most reliable and experienced firm possible. You are entitled to insist on a guarantee (look with distrust on any firm that refuses to give a guarantee). The usual guarantee states that if the tree dies within six months, provided it has been given reasonable care, it will be replaced at half the original cost. So the best insurance against loss of a tree is to make sure that you have a reliable firm of tree experts do the job.

Beware of the type of firm offering to sell you trees from the woods and forests at

The Pink Horsechestnut is an excellent flowering and shade tree

bargain rates. These almost invariably have the wrong root systems for moving purposes. Trees grown in the nursery originally were root pruned a number of times and will have developed a dense compact mass of roots confined within a small area.

Tree weeds

Certain extremely fast-growing trees such as the Weeping Willow, Lombardy, and Carolina Poplars, Manitoba Maple and the Chinese Elm are what we call tree weeds. It's true that they grow rapidly and provide quick shade, but they have many faults.

A **Weeping Willow** is entirely too large a tree for the average garden. Under good growing conditions it will fill the average lot 20 years after planting. Its roots will extend out as much as 200 feet to break up tile drains. The damage done would be exactly the same as if you had taken a sledge hammer and smashed them to pieces. **Lombardy and Carolina Poplars** reach maturity around 18 years of age and then gradually die over a period of time. They are soft wooded, and particularly susceptible to ice and wind storms.

Manitoba Maple is also a great tree for breaking up tile drains, and its seeds in the early spring create considerable mess. One heavy wind or ice storm can wreck the entire tree.

Chinese Elm is another quick growing tree which is easily damaged by wind and ice storms. Its roots will go out for long distances on all sides to rob the surrounding garden of plant food.

In view of their many faults, it is not recommended that any of these trees be planted unless exceptional circumstances demand a quick cover for a particularly bad eyesore.

Shade trees

Reliable fast growing shade trees — Forty years ago, it was almost impossible to recommend a fast growing shade tree that didn't have so many faults that it was hardly worth planting. Today nurserymen have developed quite a number of trees that not only grow quickly but have few faults. Most of them will grow anywhere from 3 to 5 feet in a year once they become established in your garden and it isn't long before you have a satisfactory tree large enough to add beauty, dignity and shade to the garden.

A standard apple tree makes a fine flowering tree in the garden

Moraine Locust — Is one of the best of the newest shade trees to be introduced during the past ten years. Locust trees are native to the North Eastern part of the continent and normally should make excellent shade trees for our gardens, but the big trouble with locust trees until now has been the ugly thorns which protrude from the branches. Unsightly seed pods were also a nuisance because they had to be gathered up in the Fall or Winter. The new Moraine

Moraine Locust is a worthy substitute for the American Elm

Locust trees produce neither thorns nor seed pods yet they grow more rapidly than the common type of locust, and have built-in disease resistance.

This tree grows at the rate of 3 to 5 feet per year which means that under good growing conditions it should reach 25 feet in height in about ten years, considerably faster than the average shade tree will do.

The Moraine Locust is a round-shaped tree when young but grows tall and vase-shaped as it gets older. Now that our beautiful elms are seriously threatened by the Dutch Elm Tree Disease, we can take a certain amount of comfort in the fact that the Moraine Locust makes a very satisfactory substitute. The lower branches tend to self prune as the top of the tree grows wider. This makes it a practical choice for narrow street plantings as sufficient clearance can be maintained for any type of traffic. Like the common forms of Locusts this tree is tolerant of smoke, soot and dust, making it a practical shade tree for city conditions.

Because of the vase-shaped form of the mature tree and the fine lacy foliage, enough sunlight filters through to permit

The Sunburst Locust is a beautiful ornamental shade tree

good growth of lawn grasses. The foliage is dark green and the leaves are lace-like.

Soil doesn't seem to matter too much for these new locusts. They will produce good growth whether your soil is heavy or light but like all other trees will grow much better if they get sufficient food and good moisture conditions.

The ice storms in some areas are a factor in choosing shade trees for the garden. Such storms will be no problem for the Moraine Locust because it is a hardwood with branches that bend easily under heavy strain of wind, snow and ice.

If you have a large lawn, say a half to an acre in size, then you could plant one as a specimen tree in the lawn. If not, plant to the side or the rear of the property to form a background for the whole garden.

Whatever you do, don't plant the Moraine Locust below overhead wires. If you do, you will soon have some butchering to do once it reaches the height of the wires. Remember this tree will grow 40 feet high when it reaches maturity.

The falling leaves present little or no problem as they crumple quickly making raking unnecessary and at the same time the soil gets back some valuable humus.

You can get an idea of the value of this fine new tree when you realize that it is patented and the "Moraine" trade mark is protected by law both in Canada and the United States.

Moraine Ash — Don't confuse this tree with the ordinary ash, as special breeding and selection have eliminated all the undesirable features, and so it's ideal for lawn or street planting. You will be most impressed with its attractive symmetrical shape which forms in its early growth and continues into full maturity. It will grow 35 to 40 feet high eventually.

The Moraine Ash bears small, olive green leaves which persist later in the Autumn than those of most ordinary ash trees. When they do fall, they sift through the lawn grasses and so eliminate raking. This fine new tree also features a smooth attractive bark that adds to its cleanliness and desirability.

It's reported hardy in such cold weather areas as Montana and North Dakota. Another point very much in its favour is its adaptability to a wide variety of soil conditions.

The Mountain Ash — The European Mountain Ash is one of the most popular of the smaller shade trees. This very ornamental tree of moderate growth makes an ideal lawn specimen tree. In the Spring, large, flat clusters of white flowers are produced followed by large bunches of flashy orange red berries which darken as the Summer season ends. This is the tree which causes so much comment each year; the tree that never fails to produce a crop of brilliant red berries. These can be a big factor in attracting birds to the garden. The robins in particular find the berries a tasty tidbit. Deep green, clean foliage perfectly compliments the graceful upright growth. Grows to a height of 18 feet to 25 feet, with a maximum spread of 15 feet. The Mountain Ash is not only suitable for planting in gardens, but for street planting also. Can be grown quite near flower beds without damaging nearby flowers or the lawn underneath.

Pin Oak — Most oak trees are slow growers, but the stately pin oak is the exception to the rule and is one of the fastest growing of the oak family. The foliage is rich green, deeply cut and becomes a glossy copper colour in the late Fall. It's one of the few trees that are generally disease and

Little Leaf Linden is one of the very best trees for street planting

insect free. Everyone likes its symmetrical, pyramidal form. At maturity it stands 30 to 40 feet high.

Pyramidal Oak — This striking vertical oak tree is not listed by every nursery, but the trouble you may have in finding it will be forgotten when you see it growing in your garden. It grows in the same shape as the Lombardy Poplar, but has none of its faults. The Lombardy poplar tends to grow very fast until it is about 20 years of age and then gradually dies away. The Pyramidal Oak on the other hand is more compact, slower growing and lives for a great many years. Once its leaves turn brown in the Fall, they continue to cling to the branch

The lovely Golden Chain Tree is a show plant all season

until early the next Spring, giving the tree a most attractive appearance throughout the Winter months. The fine green foliage is a joy to behold.

Little Leaf Linden — Here we have an ideal shade tree for the home garden, and one of the very best trees for street planting, as it is able to withstand the fumes, smoke and dust better than most trees. The trees are very long lived, have a dense pyramidal shape, have handsome heart-shaped foliage, and grow to 100 feet.

Each branch of the Sunburst Locust is a glowing gold color all season long

Weeping Mulberry — One of the finest of the small lawn specimen trees which only grows 6 feet high. It's sometimes called the "umbrella tree" and has long weeping branches which grow up to 5 feet in length. The fruits are tasty and edible and are attractive not only to human beings, but also birds.

European Beech — There is no doubt that the purple-leaved beech is one of the most colourful and beautiful of all shade trees. It is easily grown and long lived, growing 60 to 70 feet at maturity. The leaves come out a deep maroon in the Spring, turn gradually to a dark maroon-purple in the Summer, and in the Fall become a rich purple-brown. Shapely symmetry, growth and richness of colour add that final touch of elegance to the garden. This is not a tree for the very small garden, and even when planted in the larger gardens should be kept to the side or the rear of the property.

Sunburst Thornless Locust — The most spectacular introduction in the past few years as far as ornamental shade trees are concerned is without a doubt the Sun-

55

The Moraine Locust will grow 3 to 5 feet a year depending on soil conditions

burst Thornless Locust. It is the first new color in a hardy ornamental shade tree in many years and is another fast growing tree having few, if any, faults. Being hardwood it is much better for planting in the garden than willows, poplars, Manitoba maples; these soft-wooded trees are easily broken down in storms as they do not have the ability to withstand the onslaught of wind and ice.

The brilliant color and graceful form of the Sunburst Locust combined with its excellent pyramidal branching habit, has already won a whole host of friends and will win many more in the coming years.

The leaves are so small that they do not create a maintenance problem. They are fine enough to fall between the grass plants, thus eliminating the necessity of raking. The tips of the branches are bright golden yellow, shading to bronze at the ends and appear as if you've taken a paint brush and covered the tips of each branch with a bright gold paint. Having rich green inner foliage, the contrast from the branches make it look like a flowering tree just bursting into bloom.

What's still more important, this fine tree keeps its beautiful appearance all Summer long.

This new Sunburst Thornless Locust has been found to be extremely hardy in test plantings throughout the country! It transplants easily and is adaptable to almost any locality.

While it is a very fast grower, it will not grow out of bounds, and its eventual height at maturity is 30 to 40 feet. It makes an excellent lawn specimen shade tree, because the diameter of the trunk is very small in relation to other trees of similar height.

Home gardeners who plant this tree will find it full of dividends—beautiful, colourful, straight growing, shapely, disease and insect resistant, requiring minimum care and a worthy substitute for the stately elm.

Supplies of Sunburst locusts have been limited until recently, but now a good supply is in prospect.

Norway Maple — Talk to any nurseryman and he'll tell you that one of the biggest sellers in shade trees is the Norway Maple. It's a stately round headed tree capable of withstanding smoke, soot and other adverse growing conditions. For generations it has been recognized as one of the choicest shade trees. The leaves are dark green and very dense all over the tree. In the Fall they turn a rich yellow and orange to create an impressive sight. It's a fine, long lived and hardy tree. The Norway Maple is very hard wooded and does not break down in wind and ice storms. You'll find it a medium fast growing tree that will add real beauty to your garden. However, in making plans to set one out in your garden, remember that it will eventually grow 50 to 60 feet high and so there is no use locating it underneath public utility wires. If your nurseryman offers you a choice in height take the taller tree. You may pay a dollar or two more for it but you will get shade much more quickly.

Harlequin Maple—This is a new variegated-leaf Norway Maple. Try and visualize a tree completely covered with variegated silver green leaves. The center of the leaf is a rich green, the outside edge is silver-white. It's a moderately rapidly growing tree which develops a lovely round head. It is a rare tree seldom seen in gardens, yet is perfect for shade on the lawn. At maturity it will be approximately 40 feet tall.

Crimson King Maple — Here is a wonderful tree so colourful and beautiful that it deserves a place on every lawn. It is also a Norway Maple which came to this continent some years ago from Europe. Since then it has created the same sensation over here as it did in Europe. Its leaves are a bright purple-maroon giving an effect not unlike a Copper Beech except that the top of the branches and the new growth of leaves are much redder. This colour glistens so brightly and brilliantly in the sunshine, that Crimson King actually gives the impression of being in bloom all Summer long. The trees are extremely hardy and withstand the coldest temperatures.

It grows from 25 to 40 feet in height. Smoke, dust or gases do not have noticeable effects on it, so it will bring your garden colourful beauty for generations to come.

A Crimson King Maple has many uses: it's superb for lawns both large and small, makes a fine tree for street planting and is wonderful when used as a contrast among other trees.

Scarlet Maple (Rubrum) — Here's a shade tree that not only has bright green leaves all Summer long but whose vivid Fall colours catch everyone's attention. These colours are rich reds, crimsons,

Schwedler Maple has beautiful reddish-purple foliage during May and June

orange and scarlet, and are truly the brightest of any of the autumn colourings. This tall spreading tree prefers a slightly moist location. Height at maturity is 40 to 50 feet.

Sugar Maple (Saccharum) — Don't confuse the Sugar Maple with the Silver Maple whose Latin name is almost the same. Saccharinum is the botanical name of the Silver Maple. While the Silver Maple is a fast growing tree it's also soft-wooded and breaks down easily in ice and snow storms and so is not recommended for home garden planting. On the other hand, the Sugar Maple is a fine tree although it's rather slow growing. You'll discover it to be an excellent shade tree of upright dense

growth having excellent green leaves which turn to bright yellow and red in the Fall. This is the tree which can be tapped later in its lifetime for the sweet sap which boils down to make maple syrup. It's perfectly hardy, well branched, developing into one of the finest trees. Maturity height is 40 to 60 feet.

Schwedler Maple — During the past two decades the Schwedler Maple has become a very popular shade tree. In the early Summer it has reddish purple foliage which changes to green towards the end of June. This maple is hard wooded and has a good branching habit. It needs to be planted to the sides or rear of the property as it grows 30 to 50 feet in height.

Shade trees and a lily pond add extra beauty to a garden

Japanese Red Maple — This is a rare and colourful dwarf tree growing approximately 6 feet, sometimes used as a small shrub. Because of its slow growth it makes an excellent specimen tree or shrub for the lawn. Its foliage is never dense enough to harm the lawn and its brilliant crimson foliage never fails to attract attention. Having leaves blood red in colour there's nothing better for contrasting among the evergreens in the foundation planting or in the shrub border. The Japanese Maple does best when planted in full sun but will tolerate moderate shade. Under shady conditions the crimson colour is not nearly so pronounced.

White Birch — One of the best ways of using the beautiful white silver birch trees around the garden, is to plant them in clumps of three. Granted, a single tree is also very attractive, but a clump of three seems to add much more charm to the garden. The growth of the white birch is gracefully upright. Even in the Winter the delicate branches make a lovely silhouette against the drab colours of the other trees in the background.

It's best not to start with trees that are too large. If well fed and watered, birches are fast growers, considering the fact that they're a hardwood. Eventually they'll grow 35 to 40 feet in height, so don't plant them underneath or close to public utility wires.

Don't be disappointed if the bark of your birch trees is not always white, because often they do not reach this colour until they are about four years old. At this time a chemical change takes place enabling the bark to become white.

You can create some wonderful effects in your garden, by placing a flower bed

around a clump of birches.

In all too many cases, most people use them merely as a lawn specimen. This is a mistake, because by placing a large flower bed at the base of the clump of these white silver birches your garden can come alive with a beauty not usually seen in the garden world.

Someone has said that white birches and daffodils were created for each other. You will know this statement to be true if you

Flower borders and trees combine for garden charm

plant a big bed of Dutch Master or one of the other newer and large-flowered trumpet daffodils around the base of the trees. The bright golden yellow of the flowers makes a truly delightful contrast from the delicate white bark of the birches. An even more dramatic effect can be created with the soft pastel pinks and apricots of the new Pink Daffodils. Wild Rose and Pink Beauty are excellent for this purpose. The daffodils could be interplanted with a soft pink tulip like Rosy Wings to prolong the early Spring flowering season.

Once these Spring flowering bulbs have faded, they can be replaced with one of the newer petunias such as the delightful salmon-coloured Maytime or the free

The rich color of the Copper Beech adds a touch of elegance to any garden

As the birch trees grow larger, tuberous begonias can also be planted in the bed around the base. The partially shaded conditions created by the branches and foliage will give the begonias the shade they need in order to grow well. Again the soft pinks and the golden yellow coloured varieties of begonias will create a breathtaking garden scene.

For larger gardens and after the silver birches have been growing for several years, you could plant some bushes of the golden forsythia around the base and again create a wonderful contrast between the buttercup yellow of the forsythia and the white of the birches.

Cut leaved Weeping Birch — There is no doubt that this spectacular tree is unsurpassed by any other tree for the beauty and the grace of its drooping branches, silvery-white bark and delicately cut foliage. It will make a most splendid specimen tree that will add considerably to the value and beauty of your property. Even in Winter, without foliage the delicate weeping branches create a lovely picture. It is not too particular as to soil, but prefers a moist location and sunny spot in the garden. In planting always cut back the branches (except the leader) at least one third. As with any tree, never expose the roots to the sun or wind while planting. Spring planting is the best for these fine trees. About the only thing that could be said which is not in their favour is the fact that they are often attacked by the leaf miner and other injurious insects. Dusting or spraying several times during the gardening season with an all-purpose insecticide and fungicide will keep these under control.

Flowering shade trees

Nothing will add more beauty, charm and distinctiveness to any garden, large or small, than the flowering shade trees. Many of them seem to be especially designed for the small garden, because they don't grow very tall or cover a large area at maturity. Their average height is 15 feet.

The beautiful display of bloom in early or late Spring followed closely by fine foliage gives these trees a big advantage over the non-flowering type. Many of the low growing flowering shade trees are excellent lawn specimen trees.

RECOMMENDED VARIETIES

Flowering Crab Apple — A flowering crab apple tree in full bloom is a joy to behold in any garden. One or more of these delightful trees are a must for even the smallest garden. After the flowers fade they remain an attractive shade tree with bronze-coloured foliage. Finally, as Summer fades, they are covered with attractive fruits, many of which are edible. Another important point in their favour, is that they can be grown either as a comparatively low growing tree or as a tall shrub.

A check through your nursery catalogue will show that the trees are very inexpensive. There isn't a flowering tree that is any hardier or easier to grow. A colour range of the flowers is truly out of this world ranging from whites through brilliant pinks to ox-blood red and wine-purple. Most varieties of flowering crab apples grow to a maximum height of 15 or so feet if left unpruned, but you can keep them to any height by hard pruning. Used as shrubs, they can be kept low-growing to fit the style of the ranch style homes being built today. Crab apples can be safely planted under or close to utility lines because of their low height at maturity.

When ordering crab apples from the nursery, be sure to specify whether you want the tree or the shrub form.

They do not require any special type of soil and will grow well in ordinary garden earth. The method of planting is exactly the same as for any shade tree.

Almey Crab — There is no doubt that the Almey crab is one of the most beautiful of all the flowering crab apples. Your garden will be enriched by masses of huge flowers which are brilliant fiery crimson in colour. White markings at the base of each petal give the effect of a five-sided star. Almey grows 12 to 15 feet in height at maturity. It's a vigorous grower and soon attains just the right size for the modern ranch style home, very often blooming the first year after planting. It's perfectly hardy even in the coldest sections and thrives in full sunshine or partial shade. The brilliantly coloured scarlet fruits hang on to the branches long after the leaves have dropped and provide late Fall colour for the garden.

Strathmore Crab Tree — This is a type of pyramidal flowering crab which features glorious blossoms and handsome foliage. In

The new Moraine Ash makes an excellent lawn specimen tree

Augustine Ascending Elm

year. Fruits are small, ½ inch in diameter, and coloured an ox-blood red.

Simcoe — Is a lovely rose pink with reddish bronze foliage. Fruits are an attractive bright red and yellow.

Sisipuk — Here we have another very late bloomer, thus prolonging the flowering season. The attractive flowers are rose coloured with a white center. The ox-blood red fruits are ¾″ in diameter, hang on all winter, but are not good for cooking.

Van Essenstine — Is one of the best varieties of flowering crab apples. The growth is upright, clean, and the foliage is a glossy, light green in colour. Flowers are a double pink, being a dark pink on the reverse side, and light pink as the petals open on the inside. It is an excellent variety for cut flower purposes, as the bloom keeps well indoors. Hundreds of blooms are produced every year.

FLOWERING CHERRIES

Kwanzan — This is the spectacular flowering cherry that makes such a wonderful show every year around Washington. D.C. Trees bloom a year or two after transplanting, and grow anywhere from 20 to 30 feet tall. Double bright rose-pink flowers completely clothe the branches in early Spring. It's not hardy in all areas, so check with your local nursery or garden club before you buy.

Hisakura is one of the finer dwarf trees, and is the hardiest of all the Japanese flowering cherries. This variety grows 15 feet tall, and makes an especially good lawn specimen tree. The branches are simply smothered with double pink flowers every Spring.

early Spring you will enjoy its masses of rosy pink blossoms that literally cover the tree from top to bottom. When not in bloom the naturally ascending branches are covered with large, reddish bronze leaves that in the Fall turn to shades of brilliant orange and scarlet, accented with hundreds of miniature apples. Strathmore grows 10 to 15 feet tall in a slim symmetrical column, tapering to a point at the top. Trees are perfectly hardy and have withstood 20° below zero and still blossomed with abundance.

Aldenhamensis — Wine purple red flowers, are semi-double. The foliage is a bronze colour. Fruit is purple about ¾ of an inch in diameter.

Amisk — Early flowering with very ornamental fruit (not good for cooking). Flower is an amaranth pink with darker veins. Small rosehip-like-fruits are just as beautiful as the flowers, lasting late into the Fall.

Geneva — A dual purpose variety which bears large dark red bloom followed by lovely large dark red apples (about 1½″ in diameter). The fruit has dark red flesh, suitable for cooking and jelly.

Makamik — This variety blooms every year when all others have finished. Its colour is a deep rosy red with darker veins, and produces a big crop of flowers every

Standard apple trees are delightful when in bloom in May

60

Paul's Scarlet Hawthorn is the old-fashioned flowering tree that our parents knew and loved. This is not surprising because this exceptionally fine flowering tree produces extra large quantities of double, deep-crimson scarlet flowers, having rich green foliage which makes a wonderful background to highlight the flowers. Its long flowering period and attractive appearance after flowering makes this variety one of the best lawn specimen trees. You get extra beauty later in the season when the abundant scarlet fruit appears. This variety thrives in a number of locations, and is a wise choice for small gardens.

Magnolia — There is little doubt that the magnolias are one of the most elegant of all the flowering trees. Before the leaves appear, the trees are covered with a mass of fragrant, huge tulip-shaped flowers. These are coloured a rosy-white on the inside, and a lively pink colour on the outside. Leathery, deep green, waxy foliage follows the flowers and provides a restful mass of cool green during the remainder of the growing season. They usually start to flower the second year after planting, and will grow well in any soil having good drainage. They are not reliably hardy in the coldest areas, so check before you plant.

Golden Rain Trees are one of the best medium size flowering trees in cultivation. In mid-summer the whole tree is a cascade of golden bloom. Golden yellow flowers are borne in long chains which create a breath-taking sight when they stir in the breeze. Used as a specimen lawn tree, it will delight both you and your neighbours. This is a 30 footer.

Golden Chain Tree — Here is another dual-purpose tree which can be grown in either shrub or tree form. In June, the bright golden yellow flowers are produced in long hanging clusters, 18 to 20 inches in length, closely resembling the blooms of the wisteria. This fairly rare dwarf tree has green bark and foliage, and usually flowers the first year after planting. It is not hardy in colder areas, so check before you plant. Height is 8 to 10 feet.

Red Bud — This small tree presents a striking picture, with its clusters of rose pink flowers in the Spring. These are followed by large heart-shaped green leaves. It is very effective for group plantings in

It's hard to beat the flowering crab apple as a lawn specimen tree

61

Fruit trees reward you with beauty as well as fruit

White Flowering Dogwood — This is one of the most beautiful of our native flowering trees. Here is a superb lawn specimen tree for areas where the Winters are not too cold. It grows well in partial shade and is literally covered with large white blossoms early in the Spring. The flowering dogwood has a very long flowering period of anywhere from 3 to 5 weeks. In the Fall it again puts on a magnificent display with the foliage turning to brilliant shades of red, and at the same time the branches are covered with red berries. Trees grow 10 to 12 feet high.

Red Flowering Dogwood — Everyone should know this lovely artistic flowering tree. It produces a great profusion of large rose-red flowers in the Spring, and glossy red berries in the Fall. There are many locations in the garden where it may be planted, not only because of the exquisite red colour of the flowers, fruits and leaves, but because of its attractive and unique branching habit. 12 feet is its mature height.

corners of the garden or the shrub border. A redbud tree and a bed of yellow violas planted at its base are one of the most beautiful sights in the early Spring. Matures between 15 and 20 feet.

Purple-leaf Plum is one of the finest hardy, small flowering trees for the garden. The flowers are blush pink and are borne in great profusion in the Spring. As they fade, the purple leaves break out on the branches, and keep their colour throughout the Summer. The purple leaf plum makes an excellent contrast when planted among or in front of trees having the usual green foliage. It also makes an excellent lawn specimen tree. The maximum height is 15 feet.

Red Chestnut — In choosing an attractive shade tree for the garden, one of the trees you cannot afford to overlook is the Red Horsechestnut. Everyone knows the glorious array of white bloom that the ordinary chestnut produces, but just imagine the same tree with red flowers. It's a fairly fast-growing shade tree which is incredibly beautiful when in bloom. Flowering time is May and June and unlike the common chestnut, this tree does not bear nuts and so is very clean. Grows to about 30 feet.

A charming garden scene

62

EVERGREEN

EVERGREENS

Evergreens bring history and dignity to the garden

INTRODUCTION

The delicate tracery of twig and bough
Stands revealed against winter's frosty
sky.
Brings us the airs of hills and forest,
The sweet aroma of birch and pine;
Give us a waft of the north wind laden
With sweet brier odors and breath of
kine.

John Greenleaf Whittier

This is how one of the world's greatest poets felt about evergreens. Whether using them in the foundation planting, shrub border, as specimen trees, or as a hedge, you not only add great beauty to the garden, but also bring to it much history and dignity.

Next time you see evergreens, pause for a moment and try to realize that their ancestors were on the earth ages before man, and indeed are the oldest living things on the earth.

Sequoias growing on the mountainsides in California were large specimens at the time Moses led the Children of Israel out of Egypt towards the Promised Land. Isaiah mentioned them in the 41st verse and 19th chapter of his book when he said "I will set in the desert a fir tree and a pine".

There are other evergreens in China that are much older than those in California. In Mexico, an evergreen known as the Cypress del Tule has survived thousands of years and is now so big it throws a ground shadow covering an area of 7,200 square feet. Legend has it that Cortez and his army were able to camp beneath it on a march to the Honduras.

There is no doubt that the first Christmas tree was one of the evergreens, and from this has grown the lovely custom we now enjoy so much at Christmas time.

Evergreens in the garden not only bring beauty and softness during the Summer season, but provide the only greenery during the Winter months when the flowers, shrubs and trees are dormant. It would be very hard to match the majesty of an evergreen silhouetted against a background of fleecy white snow.

We mentioned earlier that evergreens are the oldest forms of life on earth; when planted in the garden they bestow a gracious permanence not often found with other plant life. Given good care and soil conditions an evergreen will continue to flourish and give forth year-round beauty

Evergreens come in a variety of colors to brighten the winter scene

and make really substantial savings in fuel costs.

Evergreens are ideal for using in all types of landscaping because they are so persistent, lasting from season to season and year to year. It is really surprising the variety of colors they offer at different seasons. They are also desirable because they do not grow quickly out of bounds.

There are several evergreens which will grow well when planted in the shade. For planting locations on the north side of the house, or in any spot which is quite shady, it is advisable to plant the yews or hemlocks. The spreading and low-growing evergreen known as Pfitzer's juniper or the dwarf and compact Mugho pine are admirably suited to partial shade conditions.

Many persons wish to plant evergreens on cemetery plots, and this is a wise choice on their part. They lend a unique touch of color to the dull and bleak Winter landscape, and add much overall beauty during Spring, Summer and Fall. However, before buying and planting any evergreens for this purpose, be sure to find out what cemetery regulations exist regarding private plantings. Many cemeteries regulate such

for your lifetime, that of the garden and for many years beyond.

Evergreens and their many uses in the garden

Although evergreens are widely planted in foundation beds surrounding the sides of houses, many people neglect to use them elsewhere in the garden. Tall, well-grown evergreens such as Koster blue spruce and Austrian pine planted as individual specimen trees at the back or the sides of the garden stand proud and erect presenting a picture of beauty.

Other tall growing kinds can be used to screen unsightly views or to provide an attractive and year-round background for the patio or outdoor living area.

In the colder parts, especially in the country, much more use could be made of evergreens as windbreaks, and as a real and effective form of climate control. It is a fact that evergreens or other trees, placed so they shade the west side of the house, will lower the roof and wall temperatures in the Summer as much as 20 to 40 degrees. In the Winter, the evergreens act as a windbreak,

Ageratum and other low growing flowers in the foundation bed

plantings to avoid disturbing the master landscape plan of the cemetery. You will usually discover that the officials in charge are only too happy to help you choose the right evergreens for the purpose you have in mind and to give you expert advice on their planting and maintenance. One of the best evergreens for cemetery use is the Japanese yew, with its rich, deep green color, and its ability to withstand considerable shade.

Evergreens to brighten the Winter scene

Ask the average person to state the color of evergreens, and he would immediately answer, "Green, of course". This answer would be only partially right, for while most evergreens are green in color, the needle bearing types grow in a wide variety of colors, including blue, silver, gold and lavender. When other trees are bare of leaves from the end of October to the middle of May, the evergreen takes over the coloring of the winter scene in the garden.

Planting and care of evergreens

Plan before you buy—Planting evergreens requires a lot of thought and plan-

Overplanting is a major fault in foundation beds

ning. The trees and shrubs must be for permanence, and so must be correctly placed at the start.

You must first decide on the type of ever-

greens suitable for your purpose. Find out the trees and shrubs best suited for your locality, the mature height and width of trees and the area covered by the spreading varieties at maturity. Armed with this knowledge you will soon arrive at the conclusion that in front of the average house, there is only sufficient space for six evergreens at the most. At first, this will mean there will be a number of bare spaces and large parts of the foundation wall will be visible. Have no misgivings about this as the spaces can be filled with good effect by planting annuals, bulbs, shrubs, biennials and perennials. The flowers will add color and charm to the new foundation planting.

Resist the temptation to fill the spaces with further evergreens. Over-planting evergreens, particularly in foundation plantings is probably the biggest single mistake made **in gardening by beginners. As soon as** evergreens are planted they produce a very pleasing effect; it is this effect which compels some people to buy more than is necessary.

Over-planting and the incorrect setting of evergreens can produce unpleasant effects, some bordering as nuisance. For instance,

Evergreens give a permanence not provided by any other plant life

Petunias mix well with evergreens in the foundation planting

For real satisfaction in obtaining evergreens, be absolutely sure as to your requirements and see you get the best value for your money.

Evergreens in the foundation planting

To be successful, foundation planting beds should be at least six feet wide. This is the absolute minimum, as eight to ten feet would be more appropriate. This may seem unduly wide, but the latter is within the scope of most gardens, and there are very sound reasons for the width.

Over-planting is one of the biggest mistakes made by both beginners to gardening and by unethical landscape men. It is certainly true there are more mistakes made in the foundation planting than in any other part of the garden.

Most foundation beds are far too small. Usually they consist of an oblong bed about three feet wide along the front and sides of the house. This lack of width is a very

a beautiful Blue spruce bought when 3 feet high can grow to 90 feet at maturity. Badly placed, it will obstruct the view or may foul hydro wires. Over-planted foundation plantings are monotonous and so do not display the evergreens at their best advantage.

The removal of trees can be very expensive, especially as mechanical equipment will have to be used in most cases. In many gardens, it would be difficult to move the equipment into place without some other damage to the garden.

With the exception of some species of yew, evergreens should not be pruned repressively. This is mentioned as some people may think they can successfully cut back an evergreen once it has grown too large. If you try to head back a Blue spruce, it will either die or develop a new center from one of the side limbs, thus causing the tree to grow in a grotesque shape.

Before employing a landscaping firm to set your foundation planting or other evergreens make sure you are dealing with a thoroughly reliable company. Do not hesitate to call your local horticultural club or the Better Business Bureau as any unethical practises carried out will be costly in the long run.

This is what happens when too many evergreens are planted to start

serious mistake because first of all we have to have enough room so that every evergreen can be located at least three feet from the foundation wall. Furthermore, the foundation planting has to be large enough to hold a representative selection of flowering shrubs, spring flowering bulbs, biennials such as violas and pansies, summer annuals and the odd perennial.

When the foundation bed is very narrow the evergreens are planted too close to the foundation wall. This can actually give an evergreen a "schizophrenic" personality in the Wintertime. The modern basement radiates heat through the foundation wall and when evergreens are planted only a foot or so from the wall, the root of the tree next to it senses that Spring has arrived. However the roots on the outside of the tree will be still in the grip of Winter. The root near the wall may start to grow during mild spells only to be damaged when the weather turns cold again. The heat also dries out the soil, and since evergreens continually give off moisture through their needles, even on days when the temperature falls to zero or lower, they can easily be in serious need of water in the midst of Winter.

There is another and still more important reason for not planting too close to the foundation wall. It may not be readily realized that during hot Summer days the sun's rays are reflected by house walls causing ground temperatures as high as 175 degrees one or two feet from the wall. This is only 37 degrees removed from the boiling point of water so it is no wonder that evergreens turn brown and die.

The man who has just bought a newly built house, or the person who is having trouble with evergreens, should examine the soil carefully where the foundation planting is either located or planned. All too often, when the builder or plasterer is finished with the house, any refuse left over indoors is pushed through the front doors or windows becoming mixed with the soil lying immediately in front of the house.

Building refuse almost invariably contains lime, and this is sure death to evergreens. Lime not only harms evergreens and other plants immediately after planting, but persists for a number of years.

Unless you are sure the soil around your house is good garden or farm soil, and it is free from lime and other debris, the best plan is to dig out the existing soil and replace it with a good top soil mixture. To ensure success, the existing soil should be removed to a depth of two feet. This may seem like a lot of work at the time, and it may be expensive, but in the long run it will pay off as it will save you disappointment, expense and labor over the succeeding years. Furthermore, the results will fully justify your efforts.

How to plant Evergreens — The best insurance for growing evergreens successfully is to have the soil in which they are planted composed of one third to one half humus. The top soil should not be black soil from woods or swamps, but good farm or garden top soil which can come either from your own garden or from one of the commercially prepared mixtures.

A great percentage of the evergreens sold in North America every year come from the Boskoop district of Holland where the evergreens thrive in a humus rich soil. Throughout this region the soil contains so much humus that when walking on it, one bounces as if on springs. For humus there is a wide choice of excellent materials, including materials processed from sewage, discarded mushroom manure, well-rotted barnyard manure, leaf mold, or material from the home compost heap.

The day you bring your evergreens home from the nursery or garden center is the day to plant them. However, if this is not practicable, it is possible to keep them for two or three days as long as they are kept in a shaded spot protected from the wind. Best plan is to set the tree in moist earth without removing the burlap making sure you spray or sprinkle the needles daily with water until you have the opportunity to plant them.

The planting operation for evergreens can be divided into five easy and simple steps.

1. You make a start by digging a planting hole several inches wider and deeper than is necessary to hold the burlapped ball of earth covering the roots. A planting hole two feet wide and two feet in depth is a good rule to follow as far as evergreens are concerned.

What do we mean by a burlapped ball of earth? When moving evergreens from the nursery to the garden, a ball of soil is kept

Evergreens require plenty of humus

Plant evergreens lower than they stood at nursery

this time the planting hole will be about half full of the soil mixture. Next, take the hose or the watering can and fill the remainder of the hole with water. This is done to further ensure the earth is well settled around the evergreen ball and that any possible air pockets are completely eliminated. Let the water drain completely away before filling in the remainder of the soil.

5. If you go for a walk in the woods and observe the conditions under which evergreens grow in nature you will discover that they always have a thick mulch of needles, leaves and other leafy plant materials covering the soil for a wide area from the trunk to well beyond the outer spread of the branches. This helps to keep the roots cool in summer and preserves the available. moisture in the soil.

Just as soon as you have finished planting is the time to duplicate this mulch in the garden or foundation planting. Spread a mulch of humus at least two to three inches deep and extending from the trunk to well beyond the spread of the branches. There is a wide choice of humus materials that can be used for the mulching of evergreens. All of them have equal merit as far as their

around the roots to prevent the evergreen receiving too severe a shock and setback because of the moving. The burlap or similar material is used to hold the soil in place.

Many garden centers and nurseries now stock evergreens planted in soil, soluble pots or other containers· which means they can be transplanted any time during Spring, Summer or Fall.

2. When placing the tree in the planting hole, do not remove the burlap around the ball, as it will rot away a few weeks after planting. All you need to do is to loosen the burlap around the trunk and either roll it back or cut away the top with a sharp knife. The time to do this is after setting the evergreens in place in the planting hole.

3. Evergreens should be planted just a trifle lower in the ground than they stood at the nursery. If you examine the trunk of the tree closely, you will be able to see the soil line as it existed in the nursery.

4. Fill in three or four inches of the special planting soil mixture and firm it well around the ball of earth to eliminate any air pockets. Then fill in another 3 or 4 inches of the mixture and firm as before. By

Petunias and evergreens combine for a fine display

value as mulches is concerned.

Any of the following makes a good mulch for evergreens. Peat moss, materials processed from sewage, well-rotted barnyard manure, grass clippings, discarded mushroom manure, compost, leaf mold, and vermiculite materials.

Late in the Fall these can be dug into the soil to increase its supply of humus. The following Spring a fresh mulch can be put down.

Be sure to give the evergreens a good soaking right after planting, and keep up the watering right through the first Summer. This does not mean that you should water every day, for this is bad, not only for evergreens, but for any part of the garden. A good soaking once a week is the best plan. You will be giving the evergreens a good soaking if the water penetrates to a depth of 7 or 8 inches.

Watering Evergreens—Evergreens in the home garden need to be watered regularly from May until freeze-up time.

You may contend that evergreens growing in the woods never receive any moisture except that by the rains. However, these evergreens have the advantage of having a deep, cool, moist mulch of humus extending a long way beyond the outer spread of the branches. This not only helps to preserve the moisture in the soil but also keeps the roots cool during the hot days of July and early August. We must also remember that evergreens in the woods have an extensive root system which can penetrate deeply to reach the permanent water table.

Compare these conditions with those in the average home garden. In the foundation planting they have a next-to-the-wall location where they suffer from the hot reflected rays of the sun during July and August, and are subject to the heat given off through basement walls from the furnace during the Winter.

In the garden there is usually no natural mulch to hold the moisture, and in all too many cases no other mulch is applied. The result is that when the weather turns hot, the ground dries out rapidly and easily. Under these conditions evergreens have to grow to

Evergreens need regular feeding

a considerable size before their roots will go down deeply enough into the soil to reach the permanent water level.

When you look at an evergreen, it is hard to realize that evaporation goes on through the needles of the trees all the time. By "all the time", we mean all seasons of the year, Spring, Summer, Autumn and Winter. Naturally, the evaporation is much more rapid in July and early August. What happens is this — the roots take the moisture from the surrounding soil and move it up through the trunk and branches to the needles. If there is no moisture in the soil, the needles will dry out, turn brown and fall off. This is usually the end of the tree, and no effort on your part at that time will revive it.

It is during the first two years, and particularly the first one that evergreens need watering the most. It seems likely, however, that under the adverse growing conditions which exist in the average subdivision today, evergreens need watering for their entire life.

The thing to keep in mind is that the roots must be kept moist, but not constantly wet. You use the same practise for watering evergreens as for the lawn and the rest of the garden. Frequent light sprinklings every

Alyssum makes a fine edging for the foundation bed

70

day are useless and can actually harm the evergreens. It is better to water once a week and let the moisture really soak into the ground. For evergreens it is best to remove the nozzle of the hose and allow a small stream of water to soak into the soil around each tree until the soil will not absorb any more water. This usually takes at least two or three hours.

Another good way is to use one of the plastic or canvas soakers which are set out on the ground surrounding the evergreens and which gradually releases water at a rate the soil can absorb without any run-off.

Having your evergreens go into the Winter with the roots dry can be just as harmful as lack of water during a hot July drought. Evaporation goes on continually through the needles of evergreens as we mentioned earlier. Even on a zero day the needles are still giving off moisture. This moisture was taken up from the soil by the roots and passed into the air through the needles.

Once October arrives, the tendency is to put away the hose and not do any more watering, just because the lawns do not need it. On the other hand, it is accepted fact that the last watering you give the

A foundation planting should consist of a balanced mixture of evergreens, shrubs and flowers

Evergreens can help to beautify a cemetery

day before freeze-up time can be the most important of the whole year. Unless the rainfall in October and November is frequent and heavy, keep on soaking your evergreens every week until the ground is frozen solidly.

Feeding Evergreens—Like other plant life, evergreens, to be their best must be fed at regular intervals. Feeding will enhance the appearance of the trees and bushes, make them more vigorous and the needles will stay green. Evergreens are apt to be taken too much for granted and so are often neglected when it comes to feeding, thus many unwittingly are doomed to poor health and perhaps extinction.

Established evergreens require feeding in April and again in either July or August. Use one half pound of complete plant food or fertilizer per foot of height of the tree. The best way to apply the fertilizer to the smaller evergreens is to dig a shallow trench around the outer spread of the branches. Sprinkle in the fertilizer at the one-half pound per foot rate and cover with soil. The rain, or the next time you water, will carry the fertilizer down to the roots.

It is possible to improve older evergreens by feeding. The best way to give them plant food is to use the same method as you would for feeding a shade tree. Just beyond the outer spread of the branches dig a series of holes, at least 18 inches deep, and about **two inches in diameter. Fill the holes with** a mixture consisting of half complete fertilizer and half dry soil or sand.

There may be other reasons for the lack of health of your evergreens. The abundant use of fertilizer certainly will not solve all evergreen troubles. For instance, it will not be able to counteract the bad effects of the lack of watering, a poor planting location, or too much shade.

For fertilizer, many people advocate the use of bone meal. In fact, they swear by it. You must remember that bone meal, which is high in phosphorous, is very slow-acting and will remain in the soil a long time before the evergreens receive any benefit from it. In any case, it is only one part of the three plant food elements the various shrubs, trees and evergreens need for top-notch growth. They also need nitrogen and potash to help them do their best. This is why a complete fertilizer containing all

A colorful scene

Ice storms in February or March can be particularly damaging, not only because the weight of the ice breaks down the branches, but if it turns sunny immediately after the storm the ice will act as a magnifying glass causing severe burning and browning of the evergreen needles. Pyramidal cedars in the foundation planting and shrub borders, and cedar hedges are often seriously affected this way.

It is unfortunate that evergreens do not recover from damage in the same manner as do shrubs. If a forsythia is broken, new growth starts from the old wood behind the break and soon covers any damage. Evergreens, on the other hand, rarely put out young growth from the old wood and if they do, it usually takes a long time.

Members of the yew family are able to start new wood, but even with them it takes two or three years to cover up the original break. With evergreens, all new growth is produced from the tips of the shoots, or from buds on the side shoots of the previous year's growth. If a branch is broken leaving a bare stub, it will always remain that way and become hidden only after a period of time by young growth

produced by surrounding branches.

This is also a good reason to be careful with the pruners. Mistakes in pruning evergreens will be there to haunt you for years to come.

It is a good plan after every snow storm to make a methodical tour of the garden, shaking the branches to dislodge the snow. This should be done the next morning after a snow storm or within 24 hours at the latest. Otherwise, the snow will be frozen fairly solidly and will be practically impossible to dislodge from the branches.

The best way of protecting evergreens is to erect a burlap screen on the south and west sides of the trees especially in the case of new plantings. We do this to cut down the damaging action of the winter winds and sun. Be sure to put the burlap screens in place before the ground freezes solid, or they will not be firm enough to withstand the wind for several months. An excellent method for doing this is to erect a frame of stout stakes driven firmly into the soil and then fix the burlap securely to the stakes. This is certainly preferable to wrapping the plants individually, although there may be isolated cases when

three plant food elements is always a much better bet for the home gardener.

Winter Protection

Many persons do not realize that evergreens in the garden need to have some winter protection. This is particularly true for those newly planted. You may argue evergreens in the woods do not receive any winter protection. While it is true they do not receive any man-made shields from the onslaughts of the cold wintry winds, they do get generally adequate protection from nature.

Our needle-bearing evergreens such as the Mugho pine, cedar, juniper, and yew which make up the bulk of our foundation and garden plantings will certainly need some form of protection.

Winter damage to evergreens can happen in two ways. First of all, the weight of snow on the branches after a storm can break many of them unless the snow is shaken from the evergreens right after the snowfall.

Plant low growing evergreens beneath windows

the latter method would be necessary.

Avoid being too eager to remove the winter protection in the early Spring, even though the weather appears bright and the screens seem unsightly. There is more damage done to evergreens during the late Winter and early Spring by the sun and wind than during the really cold months of January and February.

Winter Mulching—In the colder parts of North America once the ground has frozen solidly, it is advisable to place a thick mulch of hay, straw, well-rotted barn-yard manure, discarded mushroom manure or peat moss around each evergreen. Make this mulch 8 to 10 inches deep and have it extend at least two or three feet beyond the outer spread of the branches. The lighter materials such as hay, straw or peat moss will have to be weighted with a thin covering of earth, light pieces of lumber or tree branches to prevent the mulch from blowing away.

Why do we apply such a mulch? It prevents the soil from thawing and freezing during alternate cold and warm spells. Since the ground stays frozen hard, the

The stately blue spruce

wind will not be able to sway the trees back and forth and loosen the soil around the roots. During Winter, air pockets form which dry out the roots and kill the evergreens.

Most Evergreen Trees Drop Needles in the Fall— Pines and spruces drop one year's growth of needles in the early Fall. In Scotch pines, the 3-year old needles turn yellowish and then fall off. The red pine usually drops its 4-year old needles, while white pine normally keeps only 1 or 2 year's growth of needles.

The needles which are lost are those nearest the center of the tree. The younger, green needles are at the ends of the branches.

While this shedding operation is in progress, the trees often appear to be dead or dying. However, as soon as a hard wind or heavy rain occurs, the old needles are knocked to the ground and the tree again appears normal.

Unusual Summer seasons of drought or heavy rains may upset this natural process and cause more than the normal number of

A thick natural mulch protects woodland evergreens

73

The size of the cone does not depend on the size of the tree

the sugar pine.

We have previously mentioned in this book that evergreens come in many colors other than the traditional green. Their cones also vary in color, usually depending on the different stages of growth. They can be blue, green, violet, brown, gold or even bright yellow.

Junipers do not produce cones, but seeds in the form of berries. These berries are round and sometimes have a white, blue or even pinkish tint, and are about the size of a garden pea. On the other hand, the members of the yew family develop red berries, each of which contains a seed. In the odd case, the berries can be yellow instead of red in color.

Some cones are extremely long lasting and have been known to remain on the trees for as long as six or seven years. Others fall off after one or two years at the most. There are cones which have been designed by nature to seemingly explode, and thus scatter their seeds over a wide area. Other types are so tightly closed that they will preserve their seeds through a forest fire.

needles to drop. In these cases, if the tree keeps the current year's needles in a green healthy condition the tree will continue to grow next year.

Cones and Seeds of Evergreens— Out in King's County, California, not too many miles from Fresno is the Sequoia National Forest. As might be expected, here grow the giant Sequoias.

Visitors to this forest expect the cones produced by the Sequoia to be in direct proportion to their tremendous size. They often pick up large pine cones measuring as much as 20 inches in length and 3 to 4 inches in diameter thinking they grow on a Sequoia tree. This is a mistake because it acutally comes from the sugar pine. The Sequoia or redwood produces small cones, usually no more than 3 inches long and 1½ inches in diameter.

So you see, the size of the cone does not bear any relation whatsoever to the size of the tree. Cones vary in size from the tiny ones of the larch, which are about ½ inch in length, to the 20 inch ones of

Most evergreens drop their needles in the fall

Most popular evergreens

THE YEW (Taxus)

The yew family is without a doubt the finest evergreen for foundation planting purposes and does the best of any evergreen in shady conditions.

The various members of the yew family are no recent find or introduction in evergreens for we have been growing them in our gardens in many parts of the world for hundreds of years.

The Romans had a particular liking for the yews and freely planted them in their gardens. It was they who gave the family its botanical name of "Taxus".

However, the Romans were not the only ones to admire and grow this outstanding family of evergreens, for in Japan gardeners have been using them to create beauty around temples and homes for centuries.

The famed English longbow was made from yew trees and was the mainstay of English armies before the invention of gun-powder and firearms. A journey around older gardens will reveal many figures

The Yew or Taxus family is the finest evergreen for foundation planting purposes

The cones of evergreens come in assorted colors

carved in growing yews hundreds of years ago that are still alive and healthy to this day.

Recommended Varieties:

Japanese Yew (Upright, Taxus Cuspidata) (8 to 10 feet)—We can thank the Japanese for the development of one of the best of the ornamental evergreens. In 1861 the Japanese yew was first introduced to North America from Japan.

Like the other members of the yew family, the upright Japanese variety will survive and even grow reasonably well in the smoky and dusty conditions found in our larger cities. It has a beautiful

Members of the yew family can be pruned in much the same way as a privet hedge

pyramidal form with deep green foliage and makes an ideal evergreen for softening the corner of a house. The dense foliage has a remarkable ability to withstand heavy pruning and close shearing. The Upright Japanese yew is in a class by itself for foundation plantings, clipped specimen evergreens and hedges.

Japanese Yew (Spreading, Taxus Cuspidata) (3 to 4 feet) — This is the spreading form of the Japanese yew which usually branches out from the bottom with several stems which develop into a bush form. It produces rich, dark green foliage with numerous crimson red berries appearing in the Fall. The spreading Japanese yew trims very easily and forms a dense very desirable and attractive evergreen for planting under windows, and at the base of taller growing trees such as the pyramidal cedar. This evergreen flourishes in sunny and northern exposures.

Yew Hick's Pyramidal (Taxus Hicksi) (6 to 8 feet) — One of the first evergreens to choose when landscaping your garden should be Hick's yew. It is probably the best all-purpose evergreen that can be grown. The growth is upright, with a rich, dark glossy green foliage which is resistant to extreme heat and cold. It will grow either in sun or shade and makes an ideal evergreen for the north side of the house or other similar locations. It can be allowed to grow in its natural columnar way or trimmed into almost any shape. Hick's yew is by far the darkest green of any evergreen available. It is also the hardiest and the easiest to transplant of any of the yew family. It will grow 6 to 8 feet in height at maturity, but if trimmed regularly can be kept to any height over three feet. There seems to be little doubt that this variety will make the best possible evergreen hedge.

An excellent contrast can be achieved by planting a golden spreading juniper side by side with a Hick's yew. The former is very similar in habit of growth and appearance to the popular Pfitzer's juniper except for its bright golden needles.

Dwarf Japanese Yew (Taxus Cuspidata Nana) (3 to 4 feet) — Here is the hardiest and the smallest of all the yews which has a remarkable ability to with-

Members of the yew family grow quite well in dusty city conditions

stand both shade and a dusty smoky atmosphere. A little judicious pruning from time to time will keep it small enough so that it becomes an ideal evergreen for planting in large pockets in the rock garden or in foundation plantings and other areas where a dwarf tree is desirable.

Brown's Yew (Taxus Browni) (3 to 4 feet) — Brown's yew is a semi-upright vase-shaped evergreen with waxy green foliage. It is more compact, slower growing and requires less pruning than the Japanese yew. It is easily trimmed and makes a most attractive evergreen for planting almost anywhere in the garden, particularly in foundation plantings.

JUNIPER (Juniperus)

This family contains the largest group of hardy evergreens able to be grown in the garden. Not only will they thrive where the climate is cold, but will grow equally well in the warmer parts of North America.

Home gardeners everywhere favor junipers in the garden because they come in practically all the evergreen shapes, from bushy spreading plants to the tall thin columnar types.

Junipers like a location where they will get lots of sunshine and where the soil is not too heavy. Heavier clay soils can be prepared for planting this class of evergreens by digging in quantities of humus. All the junipers can be kept relatively small if need be, because they are easily pruned.

SPREADING JUNIPERS

Recommended Varieties:

Spreading Juniper (Juniperus Pfitzeriana) (4 to 5 feet spread) — There is no doubt that the green Pfitzer's juniper is the most popular and widely planted of all the spreading evergreens. Healthy and vigorous dark green foliage is produced on a compact spreading plant. This evergreen is unlike most other members of the juniper family because it will stand considerable shade, although it does its best in full sunshine. It is an excellent variety for planting underneath windows, as an accent

The spreading Japanese yew makes a fine hedge

Hick's yew is the best all-purpose evergreen for the home garden

plant at the base of tall growing trees and makes a most attractive entrance planting.

Blue Pfitzer Juniper (Juniperus Pfitzeriana Glauca) (4 to 5 feet spread) — This blue beauty is of great value in the garden. It resembles the popular green Pfitzer juniper mentioned above in every way except that it grows more compactly and the foliage is a delightful steel blue all year round. You will certainly admire the dense feathery foliage and the beautiful effect it creates in the Wintertime when there is practically no other color in the foundation planting or the rest of the garden.

Golden Tipped Pfitzer's Juniper (Juniperus Pfitzeriana Aurea) (4 to 5 feet spread) — This is a delightful novelty worthy of a place in any garden. Each year the new growth has brilliant yellow tips framing the dark green foliage. It makes a wonderful color contrast if planted between blue or green colored evergreens. There is no need to worry about its hardiness.

Old Gold Pfitzer Juniper (Juniperus Pfitzeriana Old Gold) (2 to 3 feet spread) — Is a slow growing more compact form of the Golden Pfitzer whose gold tipped branches keep their color all Winter long. It would be hard to find a more useful and more attractive low-growing evergreen. There is no better evergreen for planting in the larger pockets of the rock garden where it will bring much needed Winter color.

Andorra Juniper (Juniperus Horizontalis Plumosa) (2 to 3 feet spread)—Still more Winter color is provided by the low-growing Andorra juniper. The foliage is a bluish green color in the Summer, turning to a most charming purplish green in the Winter. It grows only six to eight inches high and spreads out very quickly. This is the ideal evergreen for covering banks which are too steep to permit mowing of grass. Also it is an attractive evergreen for the rock garden, foundation planting or for planting in clumps along the front of the mixed border where it will provide color in the Wintertime, at a time when none other is available.

Savin Juniper (Juniperus Savina) (3

to 4 feet spread) — This evergreen is very popular because of the low spreading form of its ascending branches and its consistently dark green needles which really stand out in the garden. It is a very compact evergreen requiring little trimming, and is hardy enough to stand the coldest Winters.

Blue Danube Juniper (Juniperus Blue Danube) (3 to 4 feet spread) — Here is a fairly new evergreen which resembles the Savin juniper mentioned above, but having a more horizontal or flat habit of growth. The lovely and striking blue foliage combines well with other evergreens. It is especially fine when planted alongside a Golden Pfitzer juniper.

Blue Hetz Juniper (Juniperus Glauca Hetzi) (4 to 6 feet spread) — The Blue Hetz juniper is recognized as being the fastest growing of all the junipers. It closely resembles the green Pfitzer juniper except that the extra fine foliage is silvery blue in color and it is a much faster grower. This variety makes an excellent evergreen for the foundation planting if given an occasional pruning to keep it within bounds.

The dwarf Japanese Yew is hardy

Brown's yew requires very little pruning

Tamarix Juniper (Juniperus Sabina Tamariscifolia) (3 to 4 feet spread) — The Tamarix juniper is a smaller form of the Savin juniper mentioned before, growing 8 to 12 inches in height. It features beautiful bright green foliage. It is an ideal evergreen for the front of the foundation planting and there need be little or no worry about its hardiness.

Hick's Savin Juniper (Juniperus Sabina Hicksi) (3 to 4 feet spread) — This is a fairly new Juniper that has the same growing habit as the Savin juniper and is just as hardy. However, the foliage is a silvery blue-green, more lacy and finer than the ordinary Savin. The upright feathery branches are particularly eye-catching.

UPRIGHT JUNIPERS

Recommended Varieties:

Mountbatten Blue Juniper (Juniperus Mountbatten) (6 to 10 feet) — This is a variety with a most delightful steel blue foliage. Its habit of growth is compact and pyramidal and does not require trimming. The beginner to gardening will value it because of its hardiness and rapid growth.

Red Cedar or Blue Virginian Juniper (Juniperus Virginiana Glauca) (6 to 12 feet) — This evergreen is a source of bewilderment to most people for despite its misleading name the red cedar is actually a juniper. It is one of our native evergreens and nature scattered it all over the North American continent from Canada to the Gulf of Mexico. It was one of the first evergreens to be grown in gardens on this continent. Those we buy from the nursery

have an upright growth habit which is both compact and pyramidal. The foliage is a rich silvery blue in the Summer but as Winter approaches the tips of the new foliage becomes a pinkish red in color. The red cedar requires some trimming, especially when small, to enable it to develop an attractive and compact habit of growth. It is an easily trimmed variety which combines well with other evergreens. Full sunshine and plenty of air circulation are its most important requirements. This is one of the few plants able to flourish in poor sandy or gravelly soil.

Myer's Juniper (Juniperus Squamata Meyeri) (4 to 5 feet) — Here we have an evergreen which is entirely different in habit, color and form. This beautiful vase-shaped juniper has an unusual foliage which is much admired. Its color is a striking blend of green, white and pinkish red. Because of its shape, color and extreme hardiness, it has many valuable uses in the garden.

Myer's Juniper Wilsoni (Juniperus Squamata Wilsoni) (4 to 5 feet) — This variety has the same upright bushy form and other characteristics of the Myer juniper mentioned above, but the foliage is a fine bluish green in color.

Spiny Greek Juniper (Juniperus Excelsa Stricta) (4 to 5 feet) — The Spiny Greek juniper is a superb quick growing beauty which rapidly attains a height of 3½ feet before slowing to mature. It has a most delightful dense columnar form with steel blue foliage all year round. This is another evergreen which does not require trimming. It can be planted in almost any part of the garden to provide stately beauty every month of the year.

The growth of Hick's yew is upright

Do not remove the burlap sacking before planting

Golden tipped Pfitzer's juniper has a 4 to 5 foot spread

Hill's Dundee Juniper (Juniperus Virginia Hilli) (6 to 10 feet) — Hill's Dundee juniper is a most attractive blue-green color in the Summer, turning to a lovely purplish-green in the Winter. It is a good evergreen to plant for immediate effect because it is a very rapid grower and requires little trimming. This makes it a favorite among beginners and for new gardens. Left to its own devices it usually throws a number of stems from the ground forming an erect bush. However, by limiting the growth to one stem, a fine upright form can easily be produced.

Blaauws Blue Vase Juniper (Juniperuss Blaauws variety) (4 to 5 feet)—This

is a good, dwarf, vase-shaped evergreen. The most delightful blue foliage and vase form will soon win many friends. This is not an evergreen to plant in the shade because it needs a sunny location in which to grow its best. Hardiness is no problem and wherever it is planted in the garden it will bring extra color and delight.

CEDARS OR ARBORVITAES

The arborvitaes are an extremely hardy group of evergreens and are used in gardens everywhere. One group or species of this evergreen is native to North America

The Blue Hetz variety is the fastest growing of all the Junipers

The Mountbatten juniper has delightful steel blue foliage

The Mountbatten blue juniper grows 6 to 10 feet high

The color of Meyers juniper is a striking blend of green, white and pinkish-red

The Tamarix juniper is a smaller form of the Savin juniper

while others are found in Asian countries, notably China, Japan and Korea. Both the American and the Asian kinds have numerous members to their respective families.

Recommended Varieties:

Pyramidal Cedar (Thuja Occidentalis Pyramidalis) (8 to 10 feet) — This pyramidal evergreen is one of the most popular, and is the type most often used in gardens. It is a beautiful dense growing tree which grows in an erect columnar way. Its height at maturity is an advantage as

The golden tipped Pfitzer's juniper makes a wonderful contrast

Myers juniper is entirely different in habit, color and form

Spiny Greek juniper is a quick-growing beauty

Hills Dundee juniper is a very rapid grower and requires very little pruning

it enables the tree to be used equally well in foundation, porch and bed plantings. It is very narrow and erect with a fine compact habit. Color is a lush, lovely dark green. To get best results, make sure that you plant it where it will get lots of sunshine.

American Cedar or Arborvitae (Thuja Occidentalis) (20 to 25 feet) — This is the native cedar which grows in many parts of North America. Most of the evergreen hedges which have been planted in Eastern gardens during the last half century have been composed of this hardy native cedar. It is a very versatile evergreen which can be trained either as a low hedge from 3 to 4 feet in height, or one as high as 10 to 12 feet. This type of hedge is very susceptible to damage from ice storms. As mentioned earlier in the book a storm in late February or early March will coat the needles with ice and when the sun comes out will act as a magnifying glass and seriously brown the leaves.

Cedars are found growing naturally in moist, often swampy ground, and so should not be planted in very dry soils. It is a

Thuja Orientalis, a compact, pyramidal, golden cedar

Blaauws juniper is an excellent dwarf vased-shaped evergreen

Little Champion is a fast growing globe-shaped cedar

good plan to lay one of the canvas or plastic soakers along the bottom of the hedge and let the water gradually soak into the ground for several hours. In periods when there is little or no rainfall, it is good practise to do this once a week to create the moist conditions in which the tree grows naturally. Moisture also helps to maintain the bright grassy green color of the foliage.

Wares Siberian Arborvitae (Thuja Wareana) (6 to 10 feet) — Here we have an extremely hardy evergreen which will stand the coldest climates, but requires a sunny location for best growth. It is a strong compact grower of graceful pyramidal form. When making your landscaping plans, this evergreen should be considered for the corner of the medium sized or large house. Color is a lovely grass green.

Little Champion Arborvitae (Thuja Occidentalis Little Champion) (2½ to 3 feet) — Little Champion is a superb hardy globe cedar first introduced in 1957. It is a fast growing, very hardy, globe shaped

Little Gem is fine for rock gardens

variety with a most pleasing green color. It requires no trimming and retains its rich naturally thick globe shape without shearing.

SPRUCE (Picea)

Spruces are one of the most important evergreens in Canada and the northern part of the United States. The family embraces a large number of forms. Many

The pyramidal cedar is one of the most popular evergreens in the home garden

Evergreens act as good windbreaks

Do not plant blue spruce in the middle of the lawn

The Nest spruce forms a low dense shrub resembling a pin cushion

of these trees are grown as magnificent lawn or park specimens while others are most suitable for hedges, windbreaks and general mass planting. There are also dwarf forms suitable for rock gardens and small borders which will maintain a dwarf, dense compact shape indefinitely.

They like the cold weather, so much so that some types are found growing inside the Arctic Circle. Pines will thrive in the warmer climates, but the spruces are not very much at home in the heat. They usually fail to grow well south of Oklahoma. While most varieties of spruces are native to the United States and Canada, there are some excellent types which have been imported to our gardens from Japan, Korea and other Asiatic countries.

We have been growing spruces for hundreds of years, so it is no wonder there is a wide variety from which to choose. They vary in size from dwarf kinds growing little more than 2 feet high, to veritable giants which eventually reach 120 or more feet in height. This is why it is necessary before making a purchase at the nursery or garden center to be sure to find out how high any of the spruces or other evergreens will be at maturity. It is only then you can make the correct decision as to a suitable location.

Recommended Varieties:

Koster Blue Spruce (Picea Pungence Kosteriana) (30 to 40 feet)—This is one of the most spectacular, finest and valuable of all lawn specimen evergreens. Its popularity is due mainly to its graceful form and brilliant, glistening silvery blue color.

Unless you have a very large garden or a small estate, you will have to keep the Koster Blue spruce and any of the other blues to the side or back of the garden. One of the most common mistakes is to plant

The blue spruce has graceful form

The Koster blue and other spruces cannot be repressively pruned

them on either side of the front sidewalk, about 15 feet from the house. Before long the trees will be 12 to 15 feet tall, and if left undisturbed will rapidly climb skyward. Such trees cannot be repressively pruned.

Those of you who have a Blue spruce already growing in your garden can create an eye-catching and tremendously colorful display by extending the bed surrounding the tree three or four feet beyond the outer spread of the branches. In the Fall fill the bed with a large number of golden yellow trumpet daffodils. The next Spring you will have color beyond your wildest dreams with the brilliant blue color of the needles contrasting sharply from the golden yellow of the daffodils. Once the daffodils have finished flowering, they can be replaced by any of the tall growing, large flowered, yellow colored marigolds. The best strains for this purpose would be Yellow Climax or Golden Climax.

When the middle of September arrives, the marigolds will no doubt be fading away, and can be replaced by some of the yellow-flowered hardy chrysanthemums, which can be moved from the nursery or another part of the garden in bud or in full flower with-

Shearing takes away the natural beauty from a Koster blue spruce

Evergreens have many uses in the rock garden

out harm or set-back. The chrysanthemums could be grown in the vegetable or cutting garden and transferred to the bed surrounding the Blue spruce about the middle of September. Some of the new giant-flowered Harvest mums would be ideal for this purpose.

For trees that have been in for 10 or more years and are 15 to 20 feet in height, a group of forsythia (golden bells) shrubs will also provide an exciting splash of late April and early May color.

You may ask about young trees that have just been planted. Naturally, the beds surrounding these would only extend about 2 feet beyond the outer spread of the branches, and the trumpet daffodils and other tall growing flowers would be out of proportion to the size of the Blue spruce. Here, you could plant golden yellow crocuses and have the same striking color effect. These could be followed by the extremely dwarf growing Petite Gold or Petite Yellow marigolds

Blue Colorado Spruce (Picea Pungence Glauca) (30 to 40 feet)—Here is an especially fine evergreen which will add

Typical farm land in Cape Breton

Norway spruce makes a fine ornamental tree or windbreak

beauty and value to your property. While the foliage is an extra fine silvery blue, it must be admitted it is not quite as intense a blue as the Koster. On the other hand, the

The magnificent Norway Spruce

86

Colorado Blue spruce usually makes a slightly better shaped tree. It is very elegant when planted as a lawn specimen tree in groups of two or three, or as a tall windbreak.

DWARF VARIETIES

One of the difficulties in planting most evergreens in the larger pockets in the rock garden is to keep them confined to the pocket. They also tend to over-run the foundation planting surrounding smaller homes. A check through your nursery catalog will show that there are several kinds of dwarf spruces which will not only stay permanently dwarf, but at the same time will maintain a dense compact shape without clipping.

Hedgehog Spruce (Abies Gregoriana Veitchi) (2 to 3 feet) — You will admire the dwarf mound-like form and compactness of this evergreen. Color is an attractive green.

Nest Spruce (Abies Nidiformis) (2 to 3 feet) — An extremely low-growing and worthwhile variety which forms a low, dense shrub resembling a nest or pincushion. The branches grow close together in tight layers and form an almost impene-

trable head. There is hardly any evergreen which grows slower than the Nest spruce. It averages about 1 inch of growth a year.

Dwarf White Spruce (Glauca Conica) (3 feet)—Is another extremely slow growing compact evergreen of the pyramidal type. Foliage is an attractive grass green.

Norway Spruce (Picea Excelsa) (80 feet) — This familiar evergreen is widely planted not only in Europe, but in Canada and the United States. Many fine varieties have been developed for ornamental uses and it is excellent as a specimen tree for larger gardens, for windbreaks or park planting. The branches are quite stiff when young, but become pendulous and droopy as the tree matures. The Norway spruce is extremely tolerant of soil conditions, and will grow in both damp and dry locations. However, the soil must be well-drained. It is also quite tolerant of a sunny or shady location. The best use for this evergreen is as a windbreak.

White Spruce (Picea Abies Glauca) (60 to 70 feet) — The White spruce is a very handsome specimen tree becoming spire-like with age. Foliage is a most attractive blue-green in color. This evergreen is not too particular about whether it is planted in heavy or light, damp or dry soils. It must have a location in full sun, and there it will withstand plenty of heat and dry weather.

PINE (Pinus)

Mention of the word "pine", and the first thing to come to mind is evergreen. Many of the members of this group are suitable only for lumbering purposes, but fortunately for our gardens there are a number which have a definite place as ornamentals. Pines only thrive in plenty of light and sunshine, so if your garden is shady, this is not

Swiss Pine

White pines make an excellent windbreak

Many pines, like Pinus Strobus, make fine ornamental evergreens

the place to plant any of the pines. They also prefer a light, sandy or gravelly soil in which to grow.

Mugho Pine or Candle Pine (Pinus mughus) (2 to 4 feet)—Here we have an extremely valuable evergreen for planting either in the foundation beds or in the larger pockets in the rock garden. It originally came to North America from the mountainous sections of northern Europe. This evergreen features a dense globe shape with foliage which is a rich, bright green. All that is needed to maintain this valuable

87

Jasper Park Lodge

that your evergreen will be a perfectly symmetrical ball of green foliage.

A tall Japanese yew with two Mugho pines at its base makes an ideal combination for use as a foundation planting.

Austrian Pine (Pinus Nigra) (30 to 60 feet)—There is no doubt that the Austrian pine is one of the most excellent and handsome evergreens for this part of the world. Its compact habit, bright green glossy foliage and rapid growth make it extremely popular as a lawn specimen tree.

Scotch Pine (Pinus Silvestrus) (30 to 60 feet) — This is the evergreen used so much for Christmas trees. In growing them as Christmas trees, they should be planted 3 x 3 feet apart. However, in order to have a well shaped symmetrical tree, some pruning will have to be done the second or third year after planting, and continued annually until the tree is cut.

evergreen in a dwarf, compact form is a little pruning every year. The new growth each season is a greyish white in color, and makes the Mugho pine look for all the world as if it were a birthday cake covered with candles and given a green icing. By late June, the new growth will have developed as much as it will in the one year, and at this time the shoots should be pinched

back. The soft young shoots should be reduced to half their length in the case of newly planted Mugho pines. This will mean

Western Yellow Pine (Ponderosa) (70 to 100 feet in the east)—This evergreen is the one covering the rolling hills and mountainsides of the west.

The widely-used Scotch pine

A pastoral scene in Nova Scotia

This tall growing pine becomes very picturesque with age and is exceptionally useful for windbreaks. It prefers a sunny open location and a deep well-drained soil.

White Pine (Pinus Strobus) (100 to 120 feet)—The white pine is the beautiful native pine of the Canadian woods and is a very handsome ornamental specimen tree. It also makes a very good windbreak. White pine likes sun, but dislikes the smoky and dusty atmosphere of large cities. It is tolerant of soil conditions, providing the earth has a good moisture holding capacity and yet is well-drained.

HEMLOCK (Tsuga)

The ornamental hemlocks we grow in our gardens are either the Canadian or the Caroline hemlock. These trees have a delightful grace and very drooping and flowing branches. They have the ability to do well in the shade and they make an ideal evergreen hedge. Main thing to watch in choosing a location for hemlocks is protection from the late Winter sun. This becomes more and more of a problem the further south you go.

Canadian Hemlock (Tsuga Canaden-

Evergreens are beautiful anywhere

sis) (70 to 100 feet) — The soft texture of the foliage of this native evergreen has always made it a favorite for ornamental planting. It is also very useful as a tall hedge in sheltered positions in suburban or rural areas. The best location for this grace-

Pines in the evening

Evergreen landscape

Canadian hemlock always has soft textured foliage

handsome and graceful form and makes a very fine ornamental specimen tree. Unfortunately, it is not as hardy as it might be. For instance, it is hardy in New England, but not reliably so in Northern Illinois. It is advisable to check with your local nurseryman or garden club before you buy, or allow a landscape man to plant it for you. If your garden is quite shady, the Carolina hemlock can be the answer to your problem. It likes a rich, moist soil, so do not plant it in a light, sandy or gravelly one. Where it is hardy, it makes a very fine tall hedge.

ful tree is in partial shade where the soil is not too dry. This is not an evergreen to plant in light sandy or gravelly soil.

Carolina Hemlock (Tsuga Caroliniana) (70 feet)—This evergreen has a very

A dwarf spruce   **Pines on the coast**

Hemlocks will grow 70 feet or more in height

JAPANESE DWARF EVERGREENS

Many persons find the Japanese art of dwarfing evergreens most fascinating when seeing it displayed at flower shows and exhibitions and wonder if they could do it in their own homes. Japanese gardeners have been able to produce gnarled and twisted evergreens in pots which are truly remarkable. Some miniature trees are so perfect that except for their size they could not be distinguished from their life-sized relatives.

Space is extremely limited in Japan not only for gardening but for living and this has no doubt led their gardeners to grow these miniature evergreens. With the traditional Japanese love of beauty, they have produced trees which are a joy to see.

When first seeing these miniature trees they appear to be hundreds of years old. Some of them are, but the majority have been developed in a few seasons' growth. The average home gardener armed with the necessary knowledge can also produce these charming miniature evergreens.

First of all you need to select the correct evergreens for the job. Cypress, cedars and

Before you plant, find out how high and how broad an evergreen will be at maturity

pines can all be successfully grown as dwarf trees.

In talks with various experts, they agree that the easiest way for the average home gardener to produce a dwarf tree is to prune the roots heavily. Naturally, you will have to leave enough roots so that the seedling will remain healthy.

Notice we said seedling. The evergreens used for this purpose would be small seedlings 4 to 6 inches high, and not the regular large specimens bought for landscaping purposes. Any reliable nurseryman should be able to arrange a supply for you. These should be inexpensive and you will be able to experiment with a number of seedlings to find out just how much of the root system can be pruned away without hurting the

evergreen too much. From then on, it is just a matter of pruning heavily every time you repot. Incidentally, it is possible to grow one of these unique trees in an ordinary bulb pan, or in one of the dishes used for a cactus garden. The Japanese often make tiny slits in the bark which allows the twisting of the stems into various shapes. Wire or twine is also used to hold a twisted branch in place until it grows that way permanently. In some cases, leaves and branches are removed. In others, the branches and trunks of the trees are bent to create the illusion of great age.

It is also advisable to help the aging and dwarfing process along by very lightly pruning back the tips of the branches each time you repot.

Closely planted blue spruce

common name of this delightful broad-leaved evergreen is the garland flower. It has a spreading habit, growing 10 to 15 inches tall, and spreading to about 18 inches to 2 feet wide. The daphne produces bright pink, deliciously fragrant flowers. It is in bloom very early in the Spring and again in the Fall. There is not too much worry about its hardiness, except in areas where sub-zero temperatures are a common Winter occurrence. It needs a sunny, well-drained location, although it will do reasonably well in partial shade. Makes an excellent flowering shrub for the front of the mixed border, foundation planting, or in the larger pockets of the rock garden. It is fine for mixing with the needle leaved evergreens.

EVERGREEN EUONYMUS Winter Creeper (1½ to 5 feet)—This is a lovely group of plants which keep their bright

Evergreens and chrysanthemums create a fine display

Euonymous Emerald Pride

BROAD LEAVED EVERGREENS

In many industrial cities and towns, it is often difficult to grow the needle-leaved evergreens, such as juniper, cedar and pine. This is where the broad leaved evergreens come into their own. Also, many of them will provide an effective winter color. Quite a number of these trees that retain their leaves in the Winter are very useful low-growing plants suitable for covering slopes, too steep to use a lawn mower, for ground cover under trees and for foundation plantings around ranch style homes .

DAPHNE (cenorum) — garland flower (15 inches) — This is a real gem for the garden having evergreen foliage which persists from year to year, but is seldom grown by home gardeners. The

Euonymus Radicans has lovely dark green leaves and fine red berries

Emerald Charm has upright columnar form

evergreen foliage all year round. They require little or no trimming and are worthy of a place in any garden.

Recommended Varieties:

Corliss Hybrids—These four varieties are disease resistant, compact and bushy in habit, requiring no staking and little pruning. They have been under tests since 1934 and have survived dry Summers and severe Winters, with temperatures down to

20° below zero. The variety Emerald Cushion is not quite as hardy as the others.

Euonymus Emerald Charm (4 to 5 feet)—This handsome rather new variety has a beautiful upright columnar form with ascending branches and dark green glossy leaves. Will grow up to 5 feet high with a spread of 1½ feet. Grows dense and very compact and is wonderful for narrow places in foundation plantings, porch entrances, as a hedge plant or as a specimen in formal plantings.

Euonymus Emerald Cushion (1½ to 2 feet) — This is the baby of the Euonymus family. It is a very dwarf shrub with dense compact habit and always retains its low

Euonymous Sarcoxie makes a fine specimen shrub

Purple leaf wintercreeper Euonymous Fortunei Colorata

93

Euonymus Carrierei is very resistant to smoke and shade

wide outline with no tendency whatsoever to trail or climb. Lush green foliage crowds the plants all year, even in the Winter. It is an ideal broad leaved evergreen for the front of the border, foundation planting or in the large pockets of the rock garden. The leaves are a lovely dark green in color and leathery in texture during the growing season, and turn a bronze green in the Winter time.

Euonymus Emerald Leader (3 to 4 feet) — This is a very distinctive variety with an erect and shapely habit of growth, rather bushy and at maturity will grow 4 feet high with a spread of 2½ feet. Forms a neatly rounded bush with thick glossy leaves. You will like the way the orange colored fruits are produced in clusters. It is superb in the foundation planting where it combines well with evergreens of all types. This evergreen is sure to brighten up any landscape planting.

Euonymus Emerald Pride (4 feet) — Here we have a neat, dwarf, compact shrub almost as broad as it is tall, with heavy foliage reaching right to the ground. Under good soil conditions will grow to a height of 4 feet with a spread of 3½ feet. This is an unusually sturdy variety which is un-excelled for foundation plantings, or the shrub border. It is extremely useful as a specimen shrub where dwarf or semi-dwarf evergreens are desired.

Euonymus Fortunei Carrierei (3 feet) — This evergreen shrub with its lustrous green leaves should be planted for Winter effect. It grows into a mound 3 feet high and is very resistant to smoke and shade, and so makes a very good broad leaved evergreen for city plantings.

Hollies make a fine show whether in leaf or in berry

Big clusters of flowers cover the Mountain Laurel bushes

across. The leaves are glossy and grow so thick you cannot see the twigs. It is very hardy and will grow either in alkaline or acid soil, in full sun or shade. Berries are black and the leaves are dark green in color and stay on the bushes throughout the Winter. It blends well with needle leaved evergreens or relieves the bareness of other shrubs when they have no leaves during the Winter time.

Box Leaf Japanese Holly (Ilex Convexa) (4 feet) — Here we have another excellent evergreen shrub with shiny dark green, boxwood like foliage. It is excellent for planting in the foundation bed or in the shrub border.

Long-Stalk Holly (Ilex Pedunculosa) — The long-stalk holly is one of the hardiest of the evergreen hollies. The female plant bears red berries on long stalks.

KOREAN BOXWOOD (Boxus Koreana) (20 inches) — The Korean box is one of our most valuable broad leaved

Euonymus Sarcoxie (3 feet) — One of the best of the broad leaved evergreens, has an excellent habit of growth, is very hardy and has beautiful dark green leaves. This makes a fine specimen evergreen in the shrub border or foundation planting, or as a medium height hedge.

Euonymus Vegetus (Climbs to 20 feet) — This is at its best as an evergreen vine for walls, as a ground cover under trees, and as a low mound in the front of the foundation planting or mixed border. The beautiful lustrous green foliage is maintained all Winter long. It prefers a northern or eastern exposure and will grow in a wide variety of soil conditions.

HOLLIES (Ilex) — The following varieties of holly are reasonably hardy maintaining their green foliage throughout the Winter. They are a welcome addition to our very short list of hardy broad-leaved evergreens.

Japanese Holly (Ilex Crenata) (3 to 4 feet) — This is a small growing holly which will be 4 feet at maturity and 3 feet

The English Boxwood is not reliably hardy when the temperature falls to zero in the winter

Yucca or Candle of Our Lord, keeps its evergreen leaves the year round

transform bare, shady spots into places of beauty. Big clusters of flowers, varying from deep rose to pure white up to 6 inches in diameter almost completely cover the lush evergreen leathery foliage. The Mountain Laurel is thoroughly hardy and makes a well formed shrub 6 to 8 feet tall under good growing conditions. About the only problem with this plant is its need for acid soil. Make the soil in which it is planted half peat moss and your plant should flourish.

YUCCA (Candle of our Lord or Adam's Needle)

Members of this Yucca family sometimes grow 30 feet high in warmer climates, but in the colder areas, the maximum height usually ranges between 4 to 8 feet.

This rather stately perennial has stiff evergreen, sword-like leaves which are produced in a cluster.

Yuccas are fine for bold sub-tropical effects, and because of their height, they need planting at the back of the mixed or perennial border. They will thrive in a variety of well-drained soils, but grow best where the soil is sandy and dry. Give them a sunny location.

Filamentosa is the variety usually grown in the home garden. The attractive plants have a striking, exotic appearance, and from their centres they thrust huge spikes of creamy white, pendulant, bell-shaped flowers. You might say that these resemble huge lily-of-the-valley, and some of them shed a heavy fragrance when open at night.

PYRACANTHA (Firethorn)

— The Pyracantha is one of the most exciting, and remarkable fruiting shrubs which keeps its evergreen foliage all Winter long. In the late Spring, large trusses of white flowers are produced and these are followed by an abundance of brilliant orange-scarlet berries which remain until late Winter. If you were to trace back its history, you would find it is actually a member of the rose family.

Some Yuccas grow up to 30 feet

evergreens. This new variety increases its popularity every year because of its hardiness. If planted in good soil conditions, it will grow 20 inches high, but can be kept to almost any level by pruning. It makes a beautiful dwarf hedge, or is very useful as an edging evergreen. This is the plant to use in city areas because it easily withstands smoke, shade and insect pests. It can be trimmed to almost any shape. The Korean box also makes an excellent specimen plant in foundation beds or borders.

MOUNTAIN LAUREL (Kalmia Latifolia) (6 to 8 feet)

— The Mountain Laurel is a native North American shrub of compact habit which has the ability to

The Mountain Laurel

Pyracantha is an extremely good plant for the foundation planting where the soil is dry. A good location would be at the front of a house which faces south. The long vines can be trained up the side of a wall, over a doorway, or along a window casing. They are easily trimmed to fit almost any position.

Field grown or large plants of Pyracantha are difficult to transplant, so it is a good idea to buy them set in six or eight inch pots from the nursery or garden center.

Such plants will grow from 2 to 3 feet the first year. There is no vine or shrub which will produce such a quantity of eye-catching berries. The name "berry" is really incorrect as they are really small apples or pomes.